Dropped Out But Not Knocked Out

Dropped Out But Not Knocked Out
Series 1
Copyright © 2004 by Tongela C. Clark
All rights reserved.

1. Biography – True Story. 2. Self Help- Motivational 3. Christian- Religion 4.Success
I. Author: Tongela Clark II. Dropped Out But Not Knocked Out
ISBN: Hardback 0-9760998-I-0
Paperback 0-9760998-0-2
Library of Congress Control Number 2004097970

Cover Illustration Design: Steve Garcia
Photographer: Ronald Johnson
Editor: Terry Baugh Bessard

Permission or Credits: "The Good Book" is The Holy Bible. In this book are different translation scripture quotations taken from the following unless otherwise indicated: King James, New International Version, Amplified
Author- Tongela Clark
Title of Book- Dropped Out But Not Knocked Out

Although information herein is based on the author's extensive experience and knowledge, it is not intended to substitute for the services of qualified professionals.
Printed in the United States

Publisher: Ready Writers
P.O. Box 88352
Houston, Texas 77288-8352
www.nomoredropouts.com
713/524-3278

Dropped Out But Not Knocked Out

By

Tongela C. Clark

Foreword by Lisa Osteen Comes

2004

Dropped Out But Not Knocked Out

CONTENTS

Acknowledgements/Dedication   ix

Foreword   Lisa Osteen Comes   xiii

From Tongela's Corner   xv

Entering the Ring   xix

Round 1   Where Is My Trainer?   1

Round 2   Geared Up, Trained Up, Conditioned Up   11

Round 3   Blocking Punches   23

Round 4   Shadow Boxing   29

Round 5   Hit Below The Belt   43

Round 6   Getting Off The Ropes   55

Round 7   Who's In Your Corner?   73

Round 8   Knocked Down Or Knocked Out   83

Round 9   Victory Is Yours   89

Round 10   My Mess Is My Message   101

And the Winner Is…   109

ACKNOWLEDGEMENTS

There is no way I could possibly acknowledge everyone. Above all men and women, to the All Knowing, the Creator of All, my Lover, my #1 Friend, the Lover of my Soul: Jesus.

Jesus, thanks for allowing the test! Out of it came a Testimony. All Glory belongs to You. When I dropped out You caught me. Everywhere I go, all men and women will know it was You and not me. I could not do this without you. Thanks a billion.

DEDICATION

To my one and only love who once walked this earth, my great grandmother, Mama (Inez). What a trainer you were and still are. What you taught me still lives today. This book is for you. You helped write this book by living your life. Thanks for providing a place of training for me. No one could ever replace you. I miss you much. To Pastor Joel Osteen, thanks for telling your dad's testimony. Now, I have a testimony. Thanks for exemplifying and teaching me humility like never before and being touchable to all men. Thanks for showing me that you don't have to go to seminary to be a preacher. You are the vessel God used to stretch me to pursue my GED. Wherever I go in life I will always be a part of Joel's Army. To the entire Osteen family and Lakewood Church, you are an Oasis of Love. To Lisa Osteen Comes, thanks for the Foreword for the book, your prayers, support and encouragement. Lisa, thanks for taking out time to be a blessing to me. You are my girl. To my 1st, sweetie, cutie pie, little niece, Sache'. You are my heart. I'm paving the way for you. To my nieces-Sydnee, Shaina and Sierra. I love all of you. Make Auntie proud. Remember all of you are Leaders, Champions and Winners.

To one I can call friend, "The Story Midwife", my Editor, Terry Baugh Bessard. Thanks for holding my hand in the "delivery room". You know I screamed, kicked, cried and almost aborted. But your coaching made my delivery easier. Thanks for never saying no and never being a negative power in my corner.

Thanks to my mother, Patricia. God used you to bring me forth. Your womb is blessed. Miss you, miss your cooking and calling. You're the best.

To my grandmother, Lena. Thanks for fighting for me. Love and miss you.

To my dad (Wolfe). Though you dropped out of my life for a season, you're not knocked out. Love you man. Keep singing and telling jokes.

To my brothers, sisters and my entire family and friends, thanks.

FOREWORD

You are about to be blessed, inspired and challenged as you read Tongela's exciting story! Tongela has been a long-time faithful member of Lakewood Church. She shared her story with our congregation, but as I read her book, I learned much more about her difficult upbringing. I am amazed at Tongela's courage and steadfast spirit. Her "overcoming" attitude opened the doors for the Lord Jesus to bring favor and promotion in her life. Her story proves that all things are possible, if you put your trust in God. The Osteen family is proud of you, Tongela. We love you and know that the best is yet to come!

Lisa Osteen Comes
Lakewood Church

FROM TONGELA'S CORNER

Les Brown
Motivational Speaker, Entrepreneur, Author, Radio & Television Celebrity

"I don't know where you are right now so I want to caution you to put on your seatbelts. Tongela Clark is about to take you on a ride through various areas of her life unlike anything that you have ever experienced. I thought my life was very difficult and hard during my upbringing, however, after just reading a couple of pages in this book, I realize my life was a beautiful dream in comparison.

Tongela proves it doesn't matter what you go through in life. What really matters is what have you learned and what are you going to do about it right now. Life gave Tongela lemons starting at birth and she crushed them and made lemonade.

Today, Tongela is a positive force on the planet to be reckoned with. The ministry she has founded provides help and support for people from all walks of life. She is an electrifying speaker, dynamic author and powerful change agent.

We are all aware when things happen to you they can make you bitter or they can make you better. Because of God's grace and mercy, Tongela is a better person in spite of all the things she has gone through and because of her work, the world is a better place. To God be the glory. Tongela, you make us all proud."

Terry Baugh Bessard
Story Midwife, Writer, Artist

"'It's a fixed fight' are Tongela's words. She believes that everything that has occurred in her life from the very beginning has been a set-up, a dress rehearsal, if you will, for what she has become and where she is headed. And it is all good.

When Tongela told me she wanted to write a book and asked me to serve as editor, I didn't know much about her past. I knew her as an expert hair stylist known for growing hair. As she grew mine, our friendship also grew along with her trust in me.

Our journey to deliver Tongela's first book began one morning in a restaurant booth. I turned on my tape recorder and began to ask her questions. I only had to ask a few. Tongela was ready for her story to come forth and it seems her story knew it was time to be told. As an avid reader and cultivator of stories, I knew a good one when I heard it. The goose bumps, an accelerated heartbeat and a full disregard for the passing of time were my indicators. I knew almost immediately that her book would have a tremendously positive impact on others. In my role as editor, I have read and re-read it many times and each time I am re-inspired.

I thank God for 'setting me up' to be a part of birthing Tongela's story."

Kirbyjon H. Caldwell
Senior Pastor, Windsor Village United Methodist Church; Author, of The Gospel of Good Success; Co-Author of Entrepreneurial Faith

"Tongela Clark is one of those rare individuals who is willing to take off her mask and shed her façade so that others may benefit. In doing so, she shows us what it is like to truly be free as we submit to the will of God. Tongela has done Fifth Ward, Houston, Texas — where I also hail from — very proud."

ENTERING THE RING

When it comes to my life, Forest Gump's mama was wrong. Life is not like a box of chocolates!!! Chocolates are sweet. My life has not always been sweet. To sum it all up, it has been a fight from the moment I entered the world. I came out of my mother's womb swinging, bobbing and weaving from the doctor's first blow. It feels like I have been in a boxing ring ever since. That is why I used a boxing theme to tell my story in this book.

If you have any doubts about whether I come out the winner, let me put them to rest now. I win even though the battles have been mighty. Many people do what they do effortlessly. Not me. Everything I have done or have achieved has been a struggle. I am always fighting to live, love and eat. I have had to face pit pushers, jealous jabs, and hits below the belt. In some cases, I have been left for dead. In most cases, I had no one in my corner and no one in the stands cheering me on.

Despite my constant opponents, not only have I survived, I have overcome everything and everyone who has come against me through the grace of God. He is the one who has taken me from ghetto girl to champion, from drop-out to achiever.

Dropped Out But Not Knocked Out is not just the title of this book; it is a true description of God's work in my life. My motto is the truth will set you free. When I testify, I reveal my worst moments because people have the tendency to look at where you are today and think you have always had it going on. If you take off the mask and the costume, you see the real picture.

Behind my mask are scars from constant abandonment,

ongoing fighting, negative words, feeling unloved and unsupported, and my own self-inflicted wounds. I used to curse, steal and lie a lot to have my way. I dropped out of high school at seventeen never imagining that years later I would hide that fact behind the image of a successful businesswoman. The pain and fear I lived from hiding that secret named this book.

Dropped Out but not Knocked Out will propel you to be all that GOD wants you to be. You will recognize that your most embarrassing moments can be your most fruitful moments. Your mess may have stressed you on yesterday, but today I decree and declare it will bless you and others. Your mess can be your message.

At one time or another, we have all attempted, approached, and even pursued something that we decided to drop out of. It could have been marriage, motherhood, ministry, school, a business venture, church, or you name it. If a dropped out spirit has ruled your past and present generations, this book is for you. If you have been down in life and it feels like there is no way up or out of your setback, this book is for you.

This book will help you pronounce benedictions to bad habits and say ashes to ashes and dust to dust to your fears, envy, strife, jealousy and inability to forgive. Whatever you failed, abandoned and aborted or however you have been accused, abused, misused, you still can be used. This book will tell you "the Fight is Fixed."

The messages in this book are brought to you from GOD through me to minister to you and to cause healing in your life. Of course, there are many other good books around today. Yet, there is still only one **good book**. That book is the Bible. The Bible proclaims the Holy Word of God and His will for our lives. GOD wants you to know that no matter what you've been through or no matter where you are today, you can succeed. It doesn't matter what your mama went through. It doesn't matter what your daddy went through. It doesn't matter what you have done, or allowed others to do to you. It just doesn't matter. GOD is still faithful, and able to restore everything you feel that you have lost.

Anyone can read this book, but as you begin to read it, your life will be transformed. You may not feel you have physically dropped out of anything, but you may have mentally dropped out. And that is where the battle always starts -- in the mind where the enemy is always ready to attack. He will tell you that you can't do it. He will tell you that you're not going to make it. He knows if he can captivate and cage your mind, he can control your actions. You won't move. You won't go anywhere. You'll say you can't do it. You'll say you're not going to make it. And your actions will show it. The enemy wants to demobilize your future, vision, and destiny.

There are a lot of people who are where I was, who have a heart and desire to come out of their dropped out situation. They just need someone to be transparent about life. If I am real about what I've been through, it allows others who are struggling to say, if she overcame that, I can, too. If GOD can do that for her, a girl from the ghetto, GOD can do that for me. He is the same GOD yesterday, today, and forever.

But if you remember, the battle is not yours. GOD reigns supreme and your opponent must bow down before Him. The battle is already won in your favor. Seek GOD and acknowledge Him in all your ways, and he shall direct your path. You can make it. You can do it. Whatever dream GOD has placed in you to do can be achieved. You are not too old, or too young. I know because of where I have been, where I am, and where I am going. GOD is waiting on you. Move it!

Here is your ticket. You are invited to enter my ring with me but before we start, let me give you a few words from the corner. As you witness my life fight, you might start thinking about your own fight. You might be in a round right now that it may seem like you are losing. I want you to know that you never lose. I don't care who your opponent is or who you have for a trainer. From the first breath you take to the last, you are a WINNER.

ROUND I

Where is My Trainer?

Ring! The bell of my life goes off. It's a baby girl. The date is September 26, 1966 and the location is Hermann Hospital in Houston, Texas. Most new babies leave the hospital with their mothers when they are released but not me. I was sick with a fever so I was left behind to get well. Little did I know that it was at that point the spirit of abandonment would take hold and stay with me for years to come.

When my mom picked me up from the hospital a few days later, we went to her mother's house. My mom didn't have her own place. She was still living in her mother's house and going to college before I was conceived. When she was pregnant with me, she stayed at a home for unwed mothers in another section of Houston called Third Ward.

It was a disgrace in my family for a young person who wasn't married to get pregnant. Back then it was something you hid. You were usually sent to another city to live with another part of the family. There was some kind of excuse given for why you weren't around for several months. Once you had the baby, you would come back and the family would pretend that the new baby was somebody else's child, like a cousin's. I don't know how many people were fooled, but that is the way it was done. But not in my case. The truth was told.

My grandmother, Lena, lived in the Fifth Ward of Houston, an African-American community that had once been known as "one of Texas' most viable black communities." When I arrived there, its new name was the 'Bloody Fifth.' There were good people who lived there, but the poverty, crime and violence had taken a toll on them and on the neighborhood.

Once my mother had me, she began to do her own thing. She would go off and stay for days, come back and leave again. At some point, she left altogether but I don't really remember a whole lot about that. I knew she was my mother; she just wasn't around on a regular basis. When she did drop by, she didn't stay long. I was never allowed to go with her, probably because she wasn't stable.

My grandmother did the best she could to take care of me but she had her own issues. She was loose, what I would call an undercover lover. She was very private and didn't have many women friends. She didn't want anyone to know her business. I think it was more shame than anything. *Have you ever been there, with shame and no one to blame? If you grew up in a mess it was not your fault. If you created your mess, don't worry, be happy. Your mess can be your message.*

When I think about my grandmother I am reminded of the story in the Good Book about the woman at the well. This woman went to the well to draw water when she knew no one else would be there. She didn't want to deal with the other women because she was ashamed. She had a history. She had a reputation. She had a track record and it was not all that good. In today's terms, she would be called a hoochie-mama. But despite her mess, GOD still used her for good.

It was said that my grandmother really loved me and I know she did. She tried to do for my mom what someone had done for her. Years earlier, she had abandoned two of her own children and someone else had to take care of them. The spirit of abandonment was on my grandmother and my mother.

I left my grandmother's house when I was still a baby. It wasn't until this book was being written that I found out why. My grandmother was mentally unstable and suffered with schizophrenia. She would have her moments when she would just go off and make a big scene in the neighborhood. One day, she had one of her fits and went into a rage. Someone must have called Child Protective Services on her. They stepped in and said if no one else in the family could take me, I would have to be put up for adoption.

When I was still in my mother's stomach, her father, my grandfather, had wanted my mother to put me up for adoption as soon as I was born. The spirit of abandonment had actually been lurking like a magnet, waiting to attach itself to me before I even came into the world. Now here it was again, forcing me out of my corner into a fight.

I couldn't do anything about this fight. The best I could do was what babies do—eat, sleep and you know what else. I didn't know what was going on. All I knew was that I was in a ring with diapers on, a pacifier around my neck, and a bottle in my mouth. I didn't know if I should crawl in a corner of the ring, lie down and play sleep, or cry until someone rescued me.

I am told that I was a very happy baby. Obviously, I did not know I was undergoing a struggle of being pulled and pushed from pillar to post. So I had no fear even though the main folks who should have been in my corner where not around. My mom and dad were playing ghosts.

I know now that I was being trained to take life's punches. I pack them like a lunch box. I have realized that before I was formed in my mother's womb, my life was predestined to be a fighter. It doesn't matter what ring I'm in, what round I'm in, or what opponent is facing me. I win. And so can you.

You see, babies never stop trying to walk. They fall, get up, fall and get back up again. They never stop achieving their goal to walk. One day out of nowhere, here comes baby girl strolling across the carpet. *That's how you are going to be strolling after you win your fight.*

There will be those looking on who never thought you could win. They don't know that your last fight built character in you and made you better and stronger.

I know that when you don't know where to go or what to say it seems like you can only take baby steps because you feel you may fall down. Don't worry, just keep moving and trying. You may be an infant in knowledge. But even in that place, in your infant stages, there is provision. We all start out as lightweight fighters but if we hang tough we will find our way to heavyweight status.

My mom was nowhere to be found. My dad was lost. My parents were doing whatever they felt like doing. One thing they weren't doing was training up a child. The spirit of abandonment was alive and well. But guess what, I was alive and well, too, even though my mom and dad chose not to train, nurture, teach, change or clean up the mess they helped make. *Sometimes the people we think should be on our side are just not equipped for the team.*

Where in the world was my referee, my trainer, my promoter? Man, I was just a baby. Where was my support system? I was kicking, screaming, nodding, slobbering and smiling all at the same time. I was in a fight but I couldn't even walk or crawl. There was no preparation, no running, no walking, no push-ups, no pull-ups, no treadmill and no Gatorade - just a bottle filled with Simulax.

I'm in round one being pushed from my grandmother's house in one corner to an unknown corner. I had to keep moving to prepare for my next round. *When you are in a fight, you must keep moving in the ring of life. Whatever you do, don't stop. Give life your best shot.*

Believe it or not, I was winning the round. *The Good Book says when your father and your mother forsake you, the Lord will take you.* The Winner has been in me from birth. I was still in the ring and I had not lost hope. I was in it to win it.

My great-grandmother Inez, who I called Mama, immediately stepped in and adopted me. According to my grandfather, his mom adopted me because she did not want me to be out of the family. *You might get kicked out of your family, but you are never kicked out of life.*

I was not the first child my great-grandmother raised that was not born to her. My mom had also lived with her. My mom was my grandmother Lena's third child. The other two children had been abandoned—one was left at the hospital and the other one was put up for adoption. My mom was the only child her mother kept and the only one she acknowledged.

Consequently, I thought my mom was an only child when I was growing up. So did a lot of the family. That is, until a few years ago, when a girl walked into my house with pictures and paperwork, said her name and told me that my grandmother Lena was also her grandmother. In other words, my mom was her mom's sister. I think my grandmother gave my mom's sister away because rumor was the father was my grandmother's uncle. Here is a new opponent in the camp named incest.

My great-grandmother took my mom from my grandmother because of the abandonment of the other two children. She also took her because my grandmother would just go off and leave my mother with different people. It was abandonment, abandonment, and more abandonment.

My mom, who I called Pat, would never bring anything when she came to my great-grandmother's house. She would always come asking for this or that. Although she said she would return what she took, she never did. Mama would have to hide her money when my mom came over because she would take it and credit cards, too. She took a blank check one time and got a large amount of money out of Mama's bank account. My great-grandmother found out, but she didn't press charges.

The only time Pat would show any type of interest in me was when she brought a guy around who seemed like he was excited to meet me. She would introduce me as her daughter and act like she was a super mom. I think that behavior has passed down in our family.

Pat married several times but she didn't marry my dad. I believe she went in and out of marriages looking for love in all the wrong places. She didn't love herself enough to know that she didn't have to look for love. There was no peace within herself about herself. She was searching. But all she seemed to find was a void.

Nothing Pat started was ever completed. Nothing seemed to ever get off the ground. Nothing bore fruit. Here was the spirit of a dropout. Marriage after marriage, job after job, man after man, start up and stop, child after child, still the same old habit of dropping out.

I never was close to my mom though our relationship got better at the end. She wasn't mean to me. She just was not a mother to me. She did only what she knew to do and to me she was the best she could be. I miss her much. What she probably didn't know was that there was a generational curse of abandonment that had been passed down from her mother to her.

There was a pattern. My grandmother had three children—two girls and a boy—and gave up two. My mom had three children—two girls and a boy—and gave up two. Both my grandmother and my mom had problems. Neither one could handle pressure well, a cycle that has continued.

The cycle of abandonment was there, round after round, and fight after fight. I have seen a lot in my day. Up until I was a teenager, I did not know who my father was. The only father figure I had was my grandfather who hadn't even wanted me in the family. I had to deal with a spirit of abandonment from my mom and my dad. Those were the cards that were dealt to me yet I refused to accept them. You see, the dealer was the enemy. The abandonment, dropping out, quitting, and other unsuccessful behaviors were things that had been permitted from generation to generation.

One thing I do know is GOD will never abandon you. Even though my mom and dad forsook me the Lord had a plan. And He has a plan for you. Listen up! It may not have been your mother or father who turned away from you. It could have been your husband, wife, sister, brother, or business partner that left you for dead or broke. Your boyfriend, girlfriend, baby daddy or whoever may have kicked you to the curb. But, you are not alone. That's why I love what the Good Book says…GOD will never leave you or forsake you. When you've been dropped out, knocked out, left out and kicked out, He will never leave you out.

You may be reading this book today feeling abused, misused, and without hope. Man may say you're out. The round is over. You have lost the fight. The referee may have thrown in the towel. Yet, if there is breath in your body, there is hope. Just think about the fights in the past when the referee counted you out but you made it anyhow. So, what makes you think you are out this time around? You are equipped to survive and win. There is more in you than you think. Stop seeing yourself as a wimp and see yourself for who you are—a WINNER for LIFE.

ROUND 1 POWER PUNCHES

Abandonment

Abandonment is what life threw at me in my early rounds of life, punch after punch and blow after blow. It spread in our family from generation to generation like an airborne infection. But guess what? The cycle stops here and guess who stops it? I stop it. Keep reading and you will understand. Yes, little old me will make the difference. You see, I will not abandon any more children. I will be the best mother in the whole wide world.

Maybe you were in the ring fighting to keep your marriage alive and you thought you lost because he abandoned you and left you for dead. When he turned his back on you, you were crawling and crying on the carpet. You couldn't even walk because the blows you received left you lying face down on the canvas.

Let me tell you a secret, your now ex-spouse is not your opponent or your enemy. He was just your training tool in this fight called life. He will be the main one commentating on how good you look when the fight is really over. You will be strutting on the red carpet, wounds healed, and healthy and wealthy in your heart. You will walk over to him and hug him and whisper in his ear, "Thanks for a wonderful workout. It made me a better woman. I now feel good about myself and am doing well for myself."

Stop taking life's blows so personally. There will be many offences in life and I mean many. So get over them. Start giving your enemy your left and watch your life go in the right direction. Start turning your negatives into positives then…watch out world.

I want you to be encouraged. You may have been the one

who abandoned someone or given a child up for adoption. GOD loves you in spite of your past, in spite of your family, your background, or your race. Hold your head up. Don't worry about the mistakes you've made. Just remember that in order for us to move forward, we must first be able to release the people that have hurt us and to release ourselves. You see, the Good Book says if you forgive men of their trespasses, your heavenly Father will also forgive you.

So let it go, release it, forgive them, forgive yourself, and watch the manifestation of your Heavenly Father turn everything around for your good. You can do it. I believe in you. Today is your day.

Incest

Now this is a creepy crawler in any family. Rumor says my grandmother's uncle fathered her first daughter. The spirit of incest is a pure mess. Incest is very sneaky but it is real. Mothers and fathers, keep your eyes open. Don't go to sleep on this one or you may wake up in a state of shock.

Be mindful of what and to whom you expose your children to. Be better fruit inspectors before you trust someone with your children. Stop trying to make an apple tree bear oranges. If your grandfather touched you and your sisters and your cousins, why do you think he begs to baby-sit for you? Has he been delivered? Then do not let him do it. We must be wise.

You may have been molested or you may be the molester because the curse is growing and going from generation to generation. GOD is no respecter of persons. Repent, seek wise counseling and prepare to take steps to your healing. You can overcome anything. Make sure you are honest and upfront. Pray that GOD will send you someone you can trust and talk to. Watch for your healing to begin.

Geared Up, Trained Up, Conditioned Up

Here I am in Round 2, back in the ring in another corner. As a matter of fact, I'm around the corner from where I started. No black eyes, no busted lips, I'm just jumping and bouncing— a baby boxer on the loose. I'm here, there and everywhere.

This fight started with a new trainer. Mama was 59 years old when she adopted me and took me to her house. Can you imagine a woman her age being a full-time mommy? I finally had a qualified personal trainer. She had been in many fights of her own in her day. She was motivated and not intimidated by what she saw. "I've always heard that what you see is what you get," she told me. "But what you **say and do** is what you get." My trainer was supportive and sweet. She was small in stature, but she was a power puncher. She passed her strength on to me.

Mama and I lived in a little wooden house that my great-grandfather had built in 1925. He died in 1945. Our house was around the corner and down the street from where my grand-mother Lena lived. It was plain but clean and full of antiques. There was a garden and fruit trees in the yard. A beauty shop was attached to the house that Mama owned and operated.

My great grandmother was set in her ways. She would not allow the younger generation to persuade her to change from the way her mom had raised her. I was very sheltered. Mama wouldn't let me spend the night anywhere and didn't want kids to come stay with me, either. Back then, grandmothers wouldn't have that, much less great-grandmothers. Her rules were strict but I never saw her angry. Can you imagine a trainer not ever raising her voice? To sum it all up, she was meek but she wasn't weak.

My power-packing, pressure-punching Mama could sting like a bee but she was tiny as an ant. She wore a size four in clothes and a nine triple-A shoe. She wore really nice stuff and only shopped at exclusive stores. She made sure that I had only the finest of things, too. I was Mama's baby. One of her babies had died and she always wanted a little girl. Years earlier, she had taken my mom in and Pat became the girl she never had. When she took me in, I took over as the girl she never had.

My mom wasn't with Mama like I was with her, though. Mama and I were close. That is why my grandfather, Mama's only child and Pat's father, despised me. He was not nice to me. He would do things for the other grandchildren but not for me. He would come over to our house with gifts for everyone. I would go through the gifts and never find anything for me. I'd say to Mama, "I told you he wasn't going to buy me nothing." My grandfather's excuse was that I already had everything.

I did have a lot. Mama made sure of it. But it still hurt and even now it hurts. My grandfather was mean. He would have made a good slave driver. He was a person allowing the devil to hitchhike. Trust me; the devil took a ride for free. They both were in the ring with me, but they weren't in my corner. My grandfather couldn't see that I was a born fighter destined to win. I don't know. I guess he had black eyes from his own fights that wouldn't let him see.

My grandfather died recently at the age of 77 years old. He spent the last few months of his life in a nursing home. Although he was not nice to me growing up, I wish I could have paid for better care for him. *You see, I've turned my bitter into better.* I loved my grandfather in spite of his behavior and I wanted the best for him. Even though he fought against me as a child, as an adult I was in his corner.

If I hated all of the people who have done me wrong in my life, there would hardly be anyone left to like. *The Good Book says love covers all sin.* So, my love for them covers everything that has been done to me. See how the tables turn? Keep living and stand still. In coming rounds, I'll teach you more about your stance as a fighter. It is the key in winning.

You might be saying to yourself that my family sounds like your family or my mom is just like your mom and so on. Whether it is man or woman you think is coming against you, it is not your flesh and blood. It is the enemy not wanting you to win. That is why my dead *mess* is now a live *message* today. So stop trying to get blood from your family and friends and get free and win and live in victory.

Even though I was pushed and picked on, Mama took up for me. Being a fighter and a longtime champion herself, she always blocked the blows. She knew her son and others were wrong. I guess the reason it didn't bother her was because she would always do for me what others refused to do. Mama really picked up my slack and my lack. She would go without to make sure I had whatever I needed and more. *A good trainer will always sacrifice.* My mom and dad did not understand that concept.

Mama could make a bad situation turn into a good one. That is the mark of an excellent trainer. Sometimes, I would go in the kitchen and there wasn't anything to eat. I would tell Mama and she would go in the kitchen. When she came out, we had a full course meal. She could turn nothing into something.

In round after round of your life, you need people who will promote you, protect you, and provide for you.

My great-grandmother constantly spoke life into me regardless of how hard the last blow was that I received. She conditioned my mind to win. *The battle always starts in the mind.* Always get it in your mind to win no matter what blow you receive to the head. Many boxers get blows. We see them bleeding from cuts to their heads, their eyes, their noses. But it doesn't stop them from fighting. It is what's in your mind that matters. Program your mind to win regardless of the blows life gives you.

Although Mama wasn't what you would call affectionate, I knew she loved me. It showed in her actions. It was evident that we had a love thing going on and she always defended me. People would tell her that she gave me too much and that I wasn't going to be anything.

Everybody thought I was too fast. They would say I was too sassy, that I talked back too much. I was and I did. What would you expect from a fighter? What fighter doesn't talk noise? I was trying to make it to the next round of my life. I have always been very verbal. I would tell Mama not to let people use her. She would try to say no to them but they would eventually talk her into helping them. Most of the money Mama lent out she never saw again. She wouldn't confront them. She always tried to keep the peace.

Mama didn't like to see me get whippings and I didn't get that many. She would try to spank me but because she was older, it was kind of hard to catch me when I broke out running. Pat whipped me once. Mama let her because I had gotten kind of fast and out of hand you could say. I was in the eighth grade and I got caught in a lie about being at school. Pat made me go in the back room of Mama's house and pull off all of my clothes so she could whip me.

I was like, how was she going to come in the middle of a

round, try to act like a trainer and train a fighter? She was talking about whipping somebody and she hadn't even been around. Please tell me what was on her mind. She started whipping me and I begin to fight back for real. As far as I was concerned, she was a stranger. She was just like everybody else jumping in, screaming and trying to beat me down when they hadn't taken the time out to invest in me or just talk to me. Mamas and daddies, make sure you make major plays in your children's life, but make sure they are positive. Start out talking before beating.

I called my grandmother Lena and told her what had happened. She came to get me. She said that Pat had no business hitting me and she called the child abuse people on her. When I got back to Mama's, I told her what grandmother Lena had done. Mama told me that I better not open the door when the child abuse people came. When they knocked on the door, we didn't open it.

One thing I can say about my great-grandmother is that she never told me anything wrong about my mom. She didn't say anything wrong about my daddy. She didn't say anything wrong about my grandmother. She didn't say anything wrong about my great-grandfather. She didn't have anything wrong to say about any of them or anyone else.

If you walked into Mama's house, she would always be nice to you. Everyone knew she was a good cook. People would come by and drink coffee and eat her pound and lemon cakes. But she would look you up and down. You know how old folks would do, scope you from head to toe. I got that from her, too.

She had sharp discernment. She could tell you if something wasn't right or if something had happened. She could tell if somebody was pregnant. She would say, "That girl there is smelling her pee." Or she would say, "That girl is having sex."

She was sharp in that area. Some things that she knew she wouldn't say. But she would speak her mind from time to time.

I had some cousins and friends who went to a church down the street from our house. Mama would not let me go to that church because that was the church my mom lied and said she was going to when she got pregnant with me. Mama said, "Oh no. You're not going to come up big like your mama, lying and saying you went to church."

She told me the difference between my mom and I was that my mom would let what my great-grandmother said go in one ear and out the other. But I listened to her and I communicated with her. That is one reason why we were so close. *See, I knew at a young age in order for me to win I had to listen to my trainer.* Now let me tell you something I always listened, but I did not always obey. So some of the hard knocks I faced were from just being hard-headed and disobedient.

In my Mama's house, we prayed. Mama had us on our knees praying every night. As a child, I wasn't always that sensitive towards GOD so I would just get on my knees, say "Thank you Jesus, Amen" and get up. I grew up on prayer. I know a lot about prayer. *Prayer is the key to winning round after round, fight after fight.* I believe that is where the gift of intercession comes forth for me, because it was imbedded in me as a child. I love to pray because that is where I get my instructions.

Mama let GOD lead. Even though the time was different and the struggle was different, I think for where she was, she really was led by GOD. There was no anger in our home. The only alcohol I ever saw was whiskey that lemon and honey was added to if someone was sick. We did not have a stereo, only an AM-FM radio. When I visited my grandmother Lena's house, I heard Natalie Cole, Sam Cooke, and those kinds of singers. At Mama's, it was just Jesus and baseball.

So I've seen holiness. *You can't tell me you can't live safe and single.* When my great-grandfather passed away, no one knew of any man that was in Mama's life other than a friend of the family some people say could have possibly been a boyfriend, but no one had any details or proof. She lived her life like a champion and she trained a champion with nobody but Jesus by her side.

We didn't have a car while I was growing up. We walked or rode the bus everywhere or someone took us. When you are preparing for a fight, walking and running is good for you. Our church was about a mile or so from our house. Mama loved the pastor. She was very active in our church and we both sung in the choir. She was well respected in the community. She made herself known at the school and was active even though there was a lot she couldn't do because of her age. She would do little things like take greens from our garden to the teachers. The gift of giving was in her heart, a gift that she passed on to me.

Mama had one close friend who was my godmother. She was a registered nurse and would advise Mama about things that my great-grandmother wasn't educated about. In fact, she was Mama's trainer. Every trainer needs a good trainer. If you are a trainer to someone, make sure you keep someone in your life to help block your hits and blows.

My godmother was the one person other than my great-grandmother who I knew was always in my corner. It was she who bought me my first phone when Mama wouldn't let me talk on the phone. She taught me a lot about business and finance.

Most of what I learned about running a business, though, I learned from my great-grandmother. I spent a lot of time in her beauty shop because I had no choice. Mama wouldn't let me go in the house until she did and that was only after she finished everybody's hair for the day.

I saw Mama as a powerful businesswoman because the odds were against her. She didn't have a business plan. She didn't have any business cards. But she had a license. She had to have a license for her and for the shop. She had to take the test or she couldn't press hair. Her education was only to the third grade. But Mama was smart as a whistle and she could read like she had finished college. But you have to realize Jesus was her Master Trainer Promoter, Teacher and Developer.

What He did for her, He will do for you. So, you can stop making all those excuses about why you can't start that business, apply for that position or manifest that dream. Remember, what you say and do you get.

Mama was very popular and very good at what she did. She could grow hair, another gift she passed on to me. Women would come back to her after their hair had been taken out by perms and inexperienced beauticians. She didn't do perms but she would grow their hair back. The same thing happened to me. They came and their hair grew.

My great-grandmother was also very loyal to her clients and would go out of her way for them. I never heard her say she didn't want to see anyone coming. She got up early in the morning and worked a late day. She charged $2.50 for a press and curl. I often wondered how we were able to succeed and dress like we dressed on those prices. We wore the best stuff. We never had to beg or want for anything. It was clear the hand of GOD was in our lives. *The Good Book says He would never leave the righteous forsaken, nor his seed begging for bread.* He is faithful to His Word.

Mama taught me independence, integrity and accountability. She taught me to do what I said I was going to do. She stressed education but she didn't push me to go to college because her knowledge of college was limited. She always told me, though, that I could make it. She told me not to worry about what I had been through. She told me that I could have whatever I wanted and that there was nothing I couldn't do. I could reach for the stars and get the moon. Whatever I wanted in the sky, I could get it.

I grew up knowing that whatever I put my hands and my mind on to do, it was done. When everybody else said I wasn't going to be anything, Mama always told me I was going to be somebody. She said, "You can be anything you want to be. You are a star and you will be a millionaire." The key is I believed her. Make sure you have a strong, positive belief system in place. Even if it is just one belief. I made it with one.

So I pass Mama's words on to you. It doesn't matter what you went through growing up. *GOD can restore and repair anything.* GOD can mend your heart and heal your relationships. I am not mad at my mother because she didn't raise me. I am not mad at my dad because I didn't know who he was. I am not mad at my grandfather because he left me out. I love them all. I have forgiven everybody. I don't have hate for anyone in my family.

We must realize that there are some things we will never understand. Some people will like you, some will love you and some will hate you. Hold your head up and keep fighting. The round may end but the fight never ends. Keep pressing, punching and jabbing your way to the next round of life.

Know that you will always meet someone to help you walk through your pain. The funny thing about that is it may not be who you want or expect it to be. We must realize that GOD has a special trainer tailor-made for each one of us. Your trainer knows your weaknesses, strengths and your pressure points. I've heard that pressure can burst a pipe. I have been under much pressure and no pipes have busted yet.

What I am really saying is don't limit yourself. You never

know what you can take until you are in the battle. You may be saying that you don't have a trainer yet. For a while, I didn't have a steady trainer. When you don't have one, you have to train yourself. There is more in you than you think. There is a trainer in everyone.

Train yourself until you identify your personal trainer. That could be your husband, wife, sister, boss, children, and sometimes even your enemies. I know you are wondering how your enemies can train you. Some of my best teachings were when my adversaries came against me and pushed some button, stepped on some toes, or spoke some words that made me see and use the ability I thought I never had.

There will be some rounds in your life when you will feel like no one is in the ring on your side and you have to be your own trainer, promoter and protector. That is when you will identify your inner strengths to win and survive within.

Bottom line, you will go through something. Pain and pressure produce muscles. So, when you go through pain and pressure you are producing stamina. Certain exercises in life will train you. Certain punches will condition you. Certain blows will gear you to grow in areas that will blow your mind and the minds of everybody watching you.

The key to winning is to finish. Make sure you never give up. Do yourself and me a favor. Don't quit. Finish. GOD is our Chief Trainer and He knows what you can bear and stand under. Now if you had looked at me as a baby you might have said, "A baby can't take all that". But I am still alive, healthy and about to be wealthy because that is what is stamped in my mind. *Let's go to the next round.*

ROUND 2 POWER PUNCHES

Family Disconnect

When you are in a fight, you would think your family would be outside the ring betting on you and cheering you on. I have a lot of family members who gamble and make major bets. But guess what, no one bets on me. They'd rather bet on the Houston Rockets, the Astros or the Texans to this very day. Many were wishing I would lose and give up or throw in my gloves. My blood family wanted me to bleed inside and out. In their hearts, they desired me to hurt and not be healed.

Many blows in my life from family and others kept me separated, isolated and disconnected. I was and still am a loner. I love people so much that sometimes I think I try to give out what I did not get as a child. Watch out for those sneaky uppercuts. All I really wanted was love and unity. To this very day, I am still in the ring fighting the fight with my family

Family and friends' blows will try to take you out. Just stand. Keep your hands up to block the blows to your head and your mind. The battle always starts in the mind. If you are disconnected from family and friends or you have been the one that has been a trouble hitter to someone else, begin to block the blows from your mind.

You see, before my family was separated in the natural, we were separated in the mind. It's like being married in the same house with your spouse, but separated and disconnected. Stand in your mind and thoughts. Be firm and secure. *The Good Book says the double-minded man is unstable in all his ways.* Be stable in your mind and watch stability manifest in your natural life.

Family Jealousy

Growing up, I received threats from many people. I cried but I learned how to ignore the noise like Mama told me to do. She told me to keep moving, that the noisemakers were jealous. They were outside the ring but I was in the ring keeping my stance. Now I must admit it hurt badly knowing that no one believed in me except Mama. When my grandfather showed love to everyone else and not me, that was like a silent blow. Silent blows can be very painful. Today, people see me standing and all they want is to see me fall on my face and fail life's race. That won't happen because there is a treasure hidden in me that makes me a winner.

There is a winner in you, also. I dare you to tap into that hidden treasure that resides in you. Rejection from family and others can cripple and handicap you from round to round in many ways, but you don't have to lose the fight. The referee won't get the chance to stand over you and count you out if you will stand, position your hands and prepare to give life your best punch.

When your family doesn't support you, it may seem like there is no one to walk with you in life. Many times the people who stood with me were not my family. From time to time, you have Seasonal Support Systems (SSS) to get you to the next round of your life. So, be very open because your SSS may step into the ring to interrupt your fight on your behalf.

ROUND 3

Blocking Punches

I met my dad in my early teens. Up until then, I had never had a hunger or thirst to see him. I had always called my grandfather "Daddy," so the daddy void had been filled to a small extent. The funny part is as I grew up, my dad would pass by our house and blow several times a week. I just didn't know he was my dad. When I met him, I told Mama, "That's the same guy who passes by all the time in that brown car."

Once I met my real father I wanted to see him more. I found out he hadn't come to see me before because my mom didn't want him to—so he says—and he didn't insist.

My mom and my dad didn't have a long relationship. It was like hit and miss. A month after I was born, he married another woman. I believe the reason my mom had not wanted my dad to see me was because she was hurt that he had been seeing another woman and wanted to get back at him. I know that was my dad's excuse. I did not live with my mom, though, and if he really wanted to see me, he could have.

It was such a battle trying to maintain a relationship with my dad, his wife and children. He was a nice man, but a weak man. He let people tell him that he couldn't see me and that I couldn't come over to his house. It was rumored that I was not his child when the truth was I looked like he birthed me instead of my mom. I believe the reason I looked so much like him was because GOD knew about the rumors before I was formed in my mother's womb.

At first, Mama thought it was good idea for my dad and me to come together but it soon became a bigger mess than before. After a while, all hell broke loose especially after he was told that I was bringing problems into his marriage. Mama stepped in and said that if my being in my dad's life was going to be a problem, then he needed to go ahead and totally disconnect from me because I was doing fine without him. She said I was not at Six Flags-AstroWorld on the Texas Cyclone going up and down all around. She didn't want me to go for any more rides on an emotional roller coaster. So, after about a year, my dad went back out of my life. It was another blow to my head and to my heart.

The man that had been missing in action, who had been in one day and out the next, was gone with the wind. From the very beginning, things got kind of windy for me from time to time. I must admit, though, that this almost knocked the breath out of me. I had let my guard down and now after the "daddy jab," my guard went back up even higher.

What I thought was a blessing turned into a messing. Being with my dad had been a temporary gain that turned into permanent pain. But I was learning how to duck and dodge with the best of them. In fact, "Ducking and Dodging" could have been my nickname.

I learned to always keep my eyes and ears open so that I would be ready for whatever came my way. In order to block punches, you must be able to hear and see them. *There are times when you will hear the enemy before you see him.* You will hear the threats and rumors before they get up on you. I have had to block many word curses and all types of verbal assassinations in my life.

The plan was to oppress, depress, discourage and intimidate me; to paralyze me mentally so I wouldn't pursue my destiny and purpose in life. My opponents wanted to demobilize me and make me inactive. As a child, the food I was served for breakfast, lunch, and dinner was: "You won't be nothing." "If something happens to Mama, I don't know who is going to keep you." "You will have to go to a girls' home if Mama dies." "You are going to get pregnant and end up just like your mother. She wasn't nothing and you won't be anything either."

Those were the kind of blows I had to block. My guard stayed up at all times. I would hear someone say one thing one minute and out of the same mouth curse me the next minute. When you go through that type of battle it is hard to trust anyone. I grew up continually wearing blockers on my hands and brakes on my feet.

As I moved out of childhood, I went from a lightweight champion to a middleweight champion. I was blessed to still have Mama as my trainer. Someone else might have walked out on me a long time before like my original trainers who walked out the very first day of my life. Mama had not given up on me. She was still in my corner, the only member of my fan club. I still had victory. I had learned a few tricks to remain successful in the ring like learning how to wear a smile even when I wanted to cry. I did cry many days but I wouldn't let my opponent see me.

There will be times in your life when you will cry on the outside and on the inside. You will be hurt from mom, dad, sister, husband, wife and even children. Nobody is exempted from packing a punch. Don't focus on who gives the blow. Focus on how you receive the blow and your attitude afterwards.

Since I was now a middleweight boxer, there were some things I had to learn to put in place. I had to make sure I wore the proper shoes to stand in and they had to be shoes of peace. Sometimes my shoes got tight and they had to be loosened to maintain a good workout. I always had to check my stand and when my legs buckled from the blows, I fell to my knees and took advantage of the opportunity to pray for my opponent. I stay in the fight through prayer. As the song says, we fall down but we get up. You may get knocked down but it does not mean you are knocked out.

Reading about my pain might cause what you thought were dead issues to rise up in you. You may be the one that received pain or inflicted it on someone else. It doesn't matter. I hope you have begun to realize that if I can maximize the moment in the midst of my madness, you can, too

There is always hope. Life is not over until it is over. *As long as there is breath in your body, you have time to make a change for you and the generations to come.*

ROUND 3 POWER PUNCH

Rejection

Rejection is a killer all by itself. It doesn't need any help. Rejection desires affection, but doesn't always know how to receive it. Because of pain you may draw back and deny affection to enter. Like, if I let you in you will steal, kill or destroy me. Rejection will not let you in the house, but will stay on the porch outside and visit. Past relationships that have driven you down pain lane in your heart and mind, may cause you to put up a block against people who truly mean you well.

I had to realize that everybody was not out to kill me. Everyone did not have ulterior motives but because of my past I would not let them in. As a result, I lost some good relationships. My insecurity and lack of trust made it hard to nurture them. My excuse was all of the rejection and abandonment that had happened in my life. I wouldn't allow anyone to get close to me, ever alert that they would treat me like my past.

But I had to be real with myself, my past and even my present and get over it. I could not continue to walk around on eggshells. Everybody was not out to destroy me. Yes, my daddy, grandfather and other men, as well as women, have rejected me in more ways than one. Yes, my heart has been torn into many pieces and marred to the max. GOD has always been able to restore all the broken pieces. Even though man has damaged and demolished me inside, GOD the Potter and the ultimate Restorer of all clay, has always put me back together again.

Rejection is real to this very day. That enemy creeps up from time to time, especially when I am taking a faith walk and I have no support team. I start feeling like no one believes in me; that everyone is against me. But that is a lie from the pit of hell.

What I do and suggest that you do is be honest with yourself and others. Come out of denial and admit that rejection is lurking. Then, commit to doing something about it. Stop beating yourself up. Quit falling into self-pity. Forgive those who have persecuted, misused and abused you. If you have inflicted pain on someone else, first forgive yourself. I had to forgive myself many times. I was my own worst enemy and did not know it. I had to forgive a lot and give in more. I had to pull off the brakes and go through my healing process and trust more.

Being confident about who you are and what you were created to be fights rejection. Focus on being free and unbound and live a life of victory. It is a new day and all things have passed away.

You may be fighting in the ring right now and wondering how it will end. Believe it or not, you have control over how it will end. Whatever you say and do you get. Start doing like I still do today, declare you are a winner and you will produce many championships. There is a champion in all of us, so activate and motivate the winner seed that was planted in you from birth to produce a long and fruitful life.

Don't judge a person by his or her past like many of us do. Focus on the person's purpose. We all have a predestined purpose and that is to win. I believe in you and can't wait to hear how you turned your mess into a message and impact the world. Remember transparency produces transformation. Let's pull off the covers and come out of our closets. Let the truth be told and watch the world become whole. That is where freedom begins.

ROUND 4

Shadow Boxing

I was very sharp at a young age. Like Mama, I had strong discernment and I knew when somebody was trying to use me. Most children who live with older people usually are more mature. You miss a lot of childhood.

I was smart and popular in school. In junior high, I used to hang out with football players and other athletes. I would assist the coaches when the teams would go off to play. I have always been cool with guys. Most of my friends now are males and I am real tight with athletes. I had close female friends. They were fast like me, but they were quiet. I didn't have the appearance of being fast but I was, and sneaky, too.

In the tenth grade I got buck wild. That's when I began to really like boys. I didn't date the guys in school, though. As I got older, Mama began to let me visit my mom on weekends during the summer.

My mom was dating a guy who had a friend who played professional football. He would come by while I was there and it was no secret that he admired me.

This man was 27. I was 15, but my body was very mature. He traveled a lot and would bring expensive gifts like Gucci purses back to me. I could tell he liked me and I flirted with him, but there was no sex at the time. I liked the attention he gave me. No one like him had ever made me feel like he did and I was hungry for a male figure in my life. The only males in my life so far had abandoned or rejected me.

During the summer of my 16th year, the relationship with the football player got serious. He came after my mind, body and heart and wanted me for all the wrong reasons. He told me he was single. It wasn't until much later that I found out he was married with children. By then, there was nothing I felt I could do. I was in love with him.

I didn't know how to say no. No one had modeled for me a positive relationship with a man. My mom was often with a different man when I saw her. Mama's husband died in 1945 and she never married again. She was never seen with another man and was afraid to deal with the subject of men. She could have had some issues that I didn't know about. The only thing I heard from Mama regarding men was her constant warning not to come up pregnant like my mom did who dropped out of college when she found out she was pregnant with me.

The relationship with the football player was an abusive one to be in at such a young age. I was very wild and emotional. We had knockdown fights and I started most of them. I still have a scar on my forehead from where he hit me with the hand that his football ring was on. I received many scars but the real ones were internal and they hurt the most. Visible scars are much easier to treat. The hidden scars linger and love to play hide and please do not see me.

At age 17, I was hanging with a girl who was 27 years old. She was one of Mama's clients and Mama would let me go down to her house and spend some time. The girl would sneak me off and let me go to the park with her. I didn't look my age. I had always hung out with older people, which made me too grown for my years. I saw a lot of stuff that the average 17-year-old was not exposed to.

My girlfriend had everything. She had a nice car. She dressed good. She had all the name brand stuff. I desired nice things like her. It was around this time that I started stealing.

Now, I know you may be thinking the next time I'm in your presence you are going to hide your purse or your wallet. Let's clarify something. Stealing is stealing. When you cheat on your taxes that is stealing. Watch yourself and don't be so quick to judge. We all have skeletons in our closet. I just have a walk-in closet with the desire to leave it open so that you can walk through and see the good, the bad and the ugly.

I would steal all kinds of stuff and do all kinds of wrong things. I did not steal from a person. The only time I did was from my boyfriend and I felt like it was owed to me. I stole from retail stores even though there was no need. I had everything I wanted.

You must be careful of your surroundings and friends. It is so easy to start doing things that our friends are doing. There is strength in numbers. The more thieves I hung around with, the harder it was to stop stealing.

My friends worked. But they were pretty fast. Many of my friends came from good families but their moms did not like me. They thought I was a bad influence on their daughters but it was the other way around. I kept my actions to myself but Mama knew something was up. She would say, "I know one thing, I don't know how you're getting all this stuff but if you go to jail for stealing, you're staying in jail." I would just tell her that somebody bought the items for me.

Mama was still strict but not as much in her old age. Because of that, I got away with a lot. Our house had burglar bars on the outside windows but I still could sneak out of the house at night, which I did. When Mama found out what I was doing, she had burglar bars put on the inside of my room. My room was the only room in our house that had burglar bars on both sides of the window.

I dropped out of school in the eleventh grade at 17, the

same age my mom had me and the same age she dropped out of college. Mama was ill. She had Alzheimer's disease and other complications and she needed care. When it came to my great-grandmother, nothing and no one else mattered. If anybody was going to stick by her side, dress her, and bathe her, it was going to be me. Nobody else did it. Everybody else said I wasn't going to be anything, but when the rubber met the road, I was the one there for her.

I would say 30 percent of my dropping out of school was to take care of Mama. The other 70 percent was peer pressure and being fast. At that time, the only time I felt bad about dropping out was in church when the high school graduates were being honored. I began to get caught up in three things—pleasing me, pleasing me and pleasing me. In trying to do that, I began to hurt me, hurt me, hurt me.

The football player introduced me to the club scene because he was in them a lot and I was always trying to find and keep up with him. My mom did clubs, too. She managed several clubs so she was out there every night and knew everybody. So did I.

No one made me go out in the streets night after night clubbing. No longer was I fresh meat after visiting a few after-hours. I was 17 years old, under age at the time that all of this started. I knew how to fight the system in more ways than one. I would become friendly with the people in authority and management so I would not have to show my identification.

Being in the clubs introduced me to alcohol and drugs. Luckily, I was not impressed much like many of my friends. I had friends who snorted cocaine in my presence, which I never desired to do. I did smoke marijuana a few times but, again, was not impressed although I often received a contact by being around it. My mom smoked weed and at one time grew marijuana plants at her house. I thought it was crazy and I never spent a red cent on it. The most I would do was drink a daiquiri or wine cooler just to look sociable and hip.

My relationship with the football player led to fighting with women. Some of them came knocking on Mama's door. During one woman's visit, I pulled a gun out. Now you see I was really out to kill from fist to gun. I had lost my mind. I remember a woman filed some type of charges on me and I was served with papers. At the police station I was arrested but the charges got dismissed. The sad thing about it was the football player took the other woman's side, just like my dad would repeatedly do to me.

It didn't matter, though; I wanted that man all to myself. I didn't care about other women, his wife or children. I remember telling him to get rid of his wife and I didn't care how he did it. My heart had entered the ring and I didn't want to hear about doing the right thing. I felt like this was my fight and no one could fit the gloves but me. It was a real roller coaster ride. This man was having issues at home with his wife and I did not make it better. I found out his home phone number, called her and told her everything hoping it would quickly run her off. It didn't right away but they eventually got divorced.

I was fighting a losing battle from the get-go. The truth is, if he had left his wife for me, he would have left me for someone else. The cycle keeps going if it is not destroyed. He was never faithful to me. When I confronted him about other women, he would lie. It was lie after lie, game after game. He would make promises to me and never keep them, just like my dad had done and would do over and over. And like my dad, he said he loved and cared for me, but not enough to fight for me.

I continued to date the football player on and off for about five years. In that span of time I got pregnant more than once. He didn't want me to have any kids and I was scared of Mama.

She would have killed me if I had had a baby and it would have been a blow to her.

But, the football player still wanted the sex. He already had several children and I am sure he did not want to pay more child support. I wanted to please him plus I knew I would have disappointed Mama if I had a baby. Everybody had already predicted I would have a baby just like my mom and others did. I was determined not to give them what they wanted. So I aborted two children. It was a temporary secret that has a permanent memory.

It is amazing that where my grandmother and mom had issues with abandonment, I took it to another level with the abortions—in other words, murder. I know we don't like that word but the truth is the truth and I must call it what it is. I am not proud of it. Abandonment is to get rid of temporarily. Abortion is to get rid of permanently.

By aborting two children, I continued the same pattern as my mom and grandmother who abandoned two children and kept one. My next child will be kept and not abandoned or aborted. The buck stops here.

My story might be similar to yours. *You may be asking how to get past the abortion that is haunting you.* You may desire to have kids but have not gotten pregnant yet. Do you think you are being punished? You may have been forced to have an abortion by your parents even though you wanted to keep your child. How do you cope with that and forgive them? What if you had sex with two or more men and got pregnant and you were mentally forced to have abortions because you didn't know which man was the daddy?

You may be a man who wanted the baby but your girlfriend, mistress, wife, or lover had an abortion without your permission. You may be a pastor who has played around and found out sista' so-and-so is pregnant. You don't want to tear up your church or your home so you insist that your mistress have an abortion but she wants the baby.

We are facing this kind of pressure in our lives daily. There are decisions we must make before and after an abortion. When I had my abortions it felt like the right thing to do at the time, but the more mature I got the more my decision saddened me. It was a pain and grief just like you might feel from a sudden death.

If you are thinking about having an abortion, don't do it. There is provision from the King for kids. You may decide to give the baby up for adoption. Remember, children are a blessing.

When I broke up with the football player, I released him totally. It was a struggle, but I made it through prayer at the end. He wanted all the nice gifts back that he had given me over the years and worked through my family and friends to get them. It wasn't easy for him. Even now, he comes by. He always wants to take me out and I always tell him no.

A couple of serious relationships followed. One of them was with a guy the whole family liked, but we didn't stay together. It seemed like in every relationship, I received battle scars in the natural and in my heart. Some fights I started; some they did. I even got to the point where I would commit destructive acts to men and their property. I hurt and did not care who hurt with me. One guy made me so mad, I lashed out at his mom many times.

You see, I wasn't always forced into the ring by someone else. Some of my blows I provoked and much of my pain I caused. Some fights, I was in the ring alone, my own opponent. I was shadowboxing—fighting my own shadow. I saw myself on the ground and tried to beat the enemy in me. I wasn't hitting anything but air.

Then, I met the dope dealer. He had been in jail and was

known as a big kingpin. He also fenced jewelry. When he got out of jail, he started dealing drugs and doing really well. We had all kinds of cars—BMW, Mercedes, Cadillac—jewelry, and other material things.

It was another unhealthy relationship. He had characteristics like my father including gambling and loving women. I can remember one night in our apartment he got so mad at me that he pulled out a nine-millimeter gun and went off on me. You would have thought I would have put on a pair of Nike tennis shoes and got up out of there. But guess what, I stayed. Even catching him with another woman didn't make me leave because he was buying me lots of stuff that I wanted. I thought it was gain and all the time it was self-inflicted pain. There was no one to blame but the girl in the mirror, Tongela Clark.

When I got with the dope dealer, Mama began to have strokes often. I knew when she was going to get sick and I would get scared. For about a month, she would have a stroke every Sunday. I was still with the dealer when Mama died in 1989. After she passed, he began to sleep with a lot of women and the relationship went downhill and finally ended. He, too, wanted everything back that he had given me in the relationship including money and cars.

That is when I came to the decision that I couldn't deal with my lifestyle anymore. I had to push all the way back from all my friends and begin a new life. They thought I was trying to be better than them. That was not the point. I was trying to do better. I had already kind of stopped stealing. The funny thing about it was all my friends went to jail for stealing but me and another friend. I stopped first. Many continued and rumor has it that some are still stealing. My prayer is that they also will get free from this self-inflicted wound.

I will always remember my day of deliverance. It was a

Sunday and I wanted to go steal but I couldn't find anyone to go with me. I called one of my friends over and over but there was no answer. I had a feeling she was probably out stealing and she was. I went so far as to even drive to the store where I wanted to steal but I drove off.

Something in me just did not set right. The real deal was that my time for wounding myself was up. I went back to my apartment and tried to call my friend again but there was still no answer. About an hour later, the phone rang and it was a collect call from my friend. She was in jail. She got caught stealing at the very store I drove by but drove off from. If I had been with her, I would have been in jail with her. When I hung up the phone I fell to my knees and cried out to GOD to take away my desire to steal.

I turned on the television and Bishop T.D. Jakes was preaching on the subject of a "Satisfied Woman." From that day on I received my total deliverance. I could not tell my friends a word. So many times in the past I had said I was going to stop doing something but I only stopped temporarily. But that Sunday it was over and I never stole again. There was no counselor, no church and no jail—just faith in me to be and live a better life.

My friends and I eventually disconnected totally. I loved them and still do, but I knew I had to change. I was tired. I made up my mind to change for life and that meant everything and everybody. Yes, Tongela Clark, began to go from high roller to Holy Roller. What a name change and change of game I have undergone. I can't believe some of the stuff I did in the past. The difference between me then and now is like night and day. GOD is so awesome to take me, a mess, and turn my mess into a message.

Although I have won major fights in the past, I can still

react like an amateur. The older you get the greater the battle and the more experience you receive from your opponents. But because I had been faced with so many opponents on an everyday basis, it seemed like everybody I came in contact with was trying to steal a blow.

When you have faced a lot of pain make sure you don't run your corner crew off because you can't trust anyone and you feel like everybody wants to steal, kill or destroy you. You have to be able to identify in your amateur stages when and when not to have your guard down. Be careful, as I have to be, that you don't slash at the people that are in your corner.

ROUND 4 POWER PUNCHES

Abusive Relationships

First, are you being abused mentally, physically, emotionally or spiritually? If so, why are you allowing yourself to be a victim? No one can make you a victim. Our worst enemies are ourselves.

Is the abuse you are allowing a repeated round in your life or does love have you bound? If love has you bound, it is love for another, not yourself. Check and see if it is a generational habit. Abuse is not limited to male or female relationships but bleeds over into every aspect of life—your workplace, your family, and your friendships.

Reverse the round. Instead of considering your opponents, consider yourself only. An effective boxer concentrates on himself or herself rather than worrying about the opponent. The only thing the boxer has to know are the rules of the fight and how to win. The way you win is by loving yourself.

There are some things that we need to drop out of and an

abusive relationship is one of them. If you are dating somebody who is beating you up, you need to drop out of that relationship for good. A lot of times we stay in wrong situations. We don't know what to do or how to get out. When it comes to doing what is good for us, we are baffled.

The way to determine if a situation is good or evil is to ask yourself if it is building you or breaking you. *What does the Good Book say?* GOD told Adam and Eve not to eat from a certain tree in the Garden of Eden. What tree are you eating off of that GOD said not to? You have to determine. Only you and GOD know the plan for your life. If you know that what you are doing is not a good thing, drop out of it. Knock it out. Let it go.

You can know the fruit by the tree. Inspect your family tree. Pull, pluck and uproot all bad and corroded fruit. You see there is fruit on all of our trees. We must be good fruit inspectors and deal with the root of the matter. I had to make sure that I got the proper fertilization to produce a greater seed so that it would grow and produce greater fruit. The key is diagnosing the tree, being real and ready to deal. In doing this you may have to let some things go and that doesn't feel good. Whatever scenario you fit in, remember, it is okay to face and confront your pain and gain your mind back.

Self-Inflicted Wounds

Beware of self-inflicted wounds. They can be habitual. Because of the repeated blows, you become numb to the pain even though the wound is re-opened with each new hit and jab. The scars remain, though, and the injury may take a long time to heal. Pain and bruises can show up much later.

Self-inflicted wounds often feel good at the time of affliction. We call it justification, sacrifice or sparing someone else but we are destroying ourselves at the same time. This is not a fight but it turns into a self-crucifixion.

If you find yourself fighting your own shadow, first of all come out of denial and admit the harm you are doing to yourself. Resist, close your own fist and as you change your mind, watch things change in your life.

Abortion

Let's define abortion: To terminate or abandon; to bring to an end or conclude or to forsake or give up completely; to quit or to leave. The definition does not say that the thing aborted is ever forgotten or can be reclaimed.

What have you aborted in your life—an unborn child? Education? Marriage? Finances? Destiny? Fear is the jab that produces the spirit of abortions.

There were things I could not achieve until I could recover from past blows. Another seed would have to be implanted in order for me to have another baby. So my task for you this round is to allow another seed to be planted in your life, watered, fertilized and watch the harvest come forth. Where do you plan to start?

Dropping Out

A lot of people have done things they are ashamed of and have dropped out of situations that they haven't forgiven themselves for. There will come times in your life that you will be ashamed and you won't have anyone to blame. Who are you going to blame? I couldn't blame anybody. I couldn't blame the devil. I couldn't blame my mama. I couldn't blame my daddy. I couldn't put the blame on anybody else's back. It was really on me because I was the one who dropped out.

For many years, I put on a mask and wore it well. You

would have thought it was Halloween every day for me. I wore the costume well. One day, I realized that while I could cover the outside, I couldn't do the same on the inside. There was no mask or costume I could put on my heart. But GOD turned my shame into gain and my weakness into strength. He did it for me when I thought I couldn't make it. He will do it for you.

You may have dropped out of something—your marriage, your career, a relationship with your child or your parents, even life—but you are not knocked out. Everyone has some type of mess. Whether you are in the White House, the black house, the suburbs or the ghetto—all mess stinks.

Keep fighting but make sure you have the Master Trainer on your side. He is truly in your corner. Our past will always try to come back and haunt us. To this very day, I have to fight giving up, procrastination and dropping out.

You can make it. Remember it is a fixed fight from beginning to end. Always know this. You are not alone. I am cheering you on to win.

ROUND 5

Hit Below the Belt

Death stings and goes very deep. It is a blow that I can't describe. All I know is that it hurts. Mama's death hit me like no other death. People say giving birth to a baby is pain like no other pain in life. That's how I felt about Mama's death. I cried like never before. It was the worst blow to this day.

In the past I had often said that I wouldn't be able to take Mama's death. I wanted to go before her, because I did not think I could handle it. I literally thought I would lose my mind. We were so close that I could not imagine life without her. She was the only one who believed in me.

When the strokes became regular at the end of Mama's life, it got so bad that I told GOD I couldn't take it anymore. It was more than I could bear but I tried to hold on to her. Besides being my personal trainer, she was a mom, friend, provider, fan, prayer warrior and so much more.

I was not looking at her suffering. She was not even responding because she was a vegetable. You see, you can be living but still dead, hooked up to a breathing machine and not responding. There are people who are hooked up to life support walking and talking but still dead. Dressed up, hooked up but they never look up. I didn't want the doctors to take Mama off the machine. I kept believing and praying for a miracle. But GOD gave me the strength to begin to let her go. I stopped trying to keep her alive for my selfish reasons. That was when she died.

When Mama passed away, I remember hearing the words—"your crutch is gone." It was true. Whatever I did out in the world, I knew that I could run back to Mama. I still had a place to eat. I still had somewhere to stay. I still could use her credit cards to buy clothes. Whatever I wanted, I could run to her to get it. When Mama was living, there was unlimited access. It wasn't until she died that I realized that I really had limited access with Mama. She could only do so much for so long. When she passed away, I had no safety net. Now I had to see what I really was made of.

My grandfather thought that since he was Mama's only child, he should run things when she died. He would not let me do anything. He was in control. I missed my trainer and wanted someone in my corner again. I began to desire a relationship with my mom and dad.

My mom and I got a little closer. I tried to get in touch with my dad and the biggest mess broke out. He called me screaming and accusing me of something I did not do and he didn't even know what happened. I only wanted him to be a pallbearer at Mama's funeral. I thought that was the least he could have done. I felt like he owed her for training and providing for his child that he had abandoned.

Being the weak man that he was, he received orders from someone else and did not come to pay his respects to Mama. Maybe he had no respect. As a result, my father and I got into a bad argument and I dared him to come to the funeral even though he had no intentions of coming. I told him if he did, he would be in a casket, too. You see, all that inside pain began to come out.

Even though I had not heard bad things about my father growing up, his behavior and actions were telling the real story. And the real man began to show up. Once again, he went out of my life. I did not hear from him until I was in my late 20's.

My girlfriend let me stay with her. It was a critical point for me after Mama' death. I could have turned in the opposite direction of where I really wanted to go. But I held on. I took small steps, but I always took steps towards my dream. My girlfriend helped push me to the next level. She had her ways. She was very controlling. But she was sweet. Whatever I wanted, she was there to do.

I decided to go to back to beauty school. I had gone to beauty school in high school but because I dropped out and stayed out for so long, I lost the hours. I started taking classes at Houston Community College before I met the dope dealer. When Mama got sick and died, I had only about a month left to finish, but I stopped going. The dropout spirit was in full force. Two years after Mama's death, I got my license.

When I got my license to do hair, I started looking for a salon to rent booth space. I knew that because of the type of clientele I wanted, I had to be in a certain area. I went to a salon close to the Houston Astrodome that was 1,800 square feet. The lady who owned it told me her booth rental was $1,000 a month. At that cost, I figured I might as well get my own shop.

So I just prayed and asked the Lord if I could get a shop in that strip center. The next month I rolled by the center and that lady's shop was gone. I talked to the owners and told them I wanted to get the space but it was extremely high. I chose another spot that was smaller. When I met with the owners, I took a professional athlete with me. I wanted the owners to know that I knew people with power and money. It worked for my good. I knew how to maneuver with stuff to get what I wanted.

I always knew I would be a businesswoman and I knew I would be very wealthy, even as a child. When I played hopscotch I didn't sing what the other kids sang. I sang, "I'm going to be a millionaire, I'm going to be a millionaire." I didn't even know what a millionaire was, but I knew I would be one.

I also knew at age 16 what the vision for my life would be. I wrote it down on a piece of paper that I have to this day. It said that I would own my own business before I was 25; I would own a building before 30; and I would get a second house at 35. The last part of that dream hasn't happened yet but the dream is still alive.

The name of my salon was going to be CelebraT's (the "T" is for Tongela) because I envisioned when I was growing up that I would do hair for stars. If I was going to do some hair, I wasn't going to charge $2.50. They were going to have to pay me.

The only people I knew who would pay me what I wanted were women who considered themselves part of the middle or upper class and higher echelon celebrities. I have been blessed to have people like BET's Jacque Reid, the Houston Rockets' MVP Cynthia Cooper and many more grace my salon, even though no one was exempted from service.

I had my first shop at age 24. It felt good but it hurt that Mama had not lived to see me get my own business. Still, it was a major achievement for me. I was the youngest stylist in the strip center. I was there for five years.

I bought my first building in 1995 at the age of 29. I found it the first day I went looking. It had been a dope house and there was some work being done on it, but I knew it was the house. I had had a vision several years earlier when I was at a hair salon in the same area that I would own a building in that area, too. I knew it would be a house that I would live above, kind of like what I grew up in. I gave the realtor $1,000 earnest money on a Thursday and was pre-approved the next Tuesday for $150,000. I had never bought a house. I paid $95,000 for the house and the house was appraised in 2004 for $375,000.

I had what people would call success and I was doing well. I was 33 years old and my business was making more than

$100,000. From the outside everything looked great. No one knew I was hiding the secret of being a high school dropout. I had been able to get whatever I wanted in life. The only thing I had not been able to maneuver and talk my way into was getting a diploma and the enemy tormented me about it.

I was being beat up in my mind. I was fearful, embarrassed and ashamed, concerned about how I would look if everyone knew my failure. People may have thought I had it going on, but if they would have followed me home and pulled back the curtains of my life, they would have witnessed a river of tears. What looked like glamour on many days was actually pain and gloom.

Everybody I knew, all of my friends had degrees. I only felt powerless when people began to talk about the stuff. I would be in a group of people and they would go around the room and ask what school and what year each person attended and finished. When they asked me what school I went to, I would say Kashmere High School, which was the truth. Then, when they asked me what year I finished, I would say 1985.

That was a lie. I didn't finish. I had dropped out, remember? Afterwards when I was alone, I would feel really bad. I felt bad because I knew I had lied, and I felt bad because I hadn't finished school. It wasn't good and it didn't feel right. Just the conversation of school was a hit below the belt. That blow made me crippled yet determined at the same time.

I began to get convicted. When people started talking about school and graduating, I would leave out of the room if I could. I would either try to remove myself from their presence or the conversation or change the subject. I didn't want to lie about it. I just didn't want to deal with it.

But the enemy kept reminding me of it. I was at a church one time and another lady who was a minister there stood up and said she didn't have a high school diploma or General Equivalency Diploma (GED). I was getting ready to stand up and tell her my situation, but the pastor got up and told the woman that she had to go back and get her GED if she really wanted GOD to use her and if she wanted to go to the next level.

I didn't have a GED and I knew GOD was using me. I went to the minister afterwards and asked him how he could say that GOD wasn't going to use her to the max. I wanted to tell him that I didn't have a GED. But I could not say it.

The woman left the church a little later because she was very torn down about what the pastor had told her and other comments. That is the kind of thing that can affect your destiny and detour your dream. You see, the enemy knows who and how to hit below the belt. The enemy hit a two-for-one that time. He punched at that lady and managed to hit me with the same blow. The enemy is so strategic.

A dropped out spirit can affect your destiny, also. It is amazing when I look at how the enemy has attacked the women in my family. You can see his work in the pattern. Mama had only reached the third grade. My grandmother didn't finish school. My mom finished high school, but dropped out of college. I dropped out of high school. That spirit had been transferred from generation to generation, woman-to-woman.

But as painful as my secret was, there was another one that was about to come at me that would almost keep me down for the count. I had met a man and fell deeply in love with him. This was not a thug or a street man but a man who played golf and tennis and enjoyed skiing and participating in book clubs. He was attentive, sensitive, compassionate and responsive. He knew how to make my clock tick. I had never met a man so tuned into a woman and how to make her happy.

There was one other way this man was different from the

other men in my life. He was bisexual. I had experiences in the past with men having women on the side but this man had men on the side. How did the trickster get tricked? Even my dad had been fooled. He liked the guy. When I asked him if he thought he was gay he told me no, that the guy just had class. Everyone else—my family and friends—said they could tell he was bisexual.

I must admit that I had a feeling but I didn't want to believe it. I got too caught up in pleasing myself. I did observe little signs. The wife of one his friends revealed that she was suspicious that her husband was bisexual, too. More and more pieces of the puzzle began to come together. I confronted him about being bisexual, but he denied it. Eventually, though, it got confirmed.

Now don't frown up. This is everyday life. Many men today are living double lives. There are things that happen to us in childhood whether it is molestation, sexual fantasies or other hidden issues that cause trauma some of us never recover from. This guy wasn't a bad guy. He was and remains a jewel. He just has some mess that he has not yet turned into a message.

Nevertheless, it was a painful hit. I almost married this man and would have if we had not had some other issues. Even though he was good to me, he was not good for me because of his lifestyle. After we broke up, I was tormented like never before. I thought I had AIDS. I was so ill that whenever I tried to get up from my bed, I fell down. It was the one time my mom and dad came together. They took care of me on my sickbed.

The relationship scared me for years but the pain helped begin to break the cycle of looking for love in the wrong places for the wrong reasons. I had been seeking a trainer in the men I brought into my life and none of them measured up. After that, I began to abstain from sex.

I have since learned to love people where they are and to not be judgmental. We all have some type of mess in our lives. I just chose to turn my mess into a message. I am not the same person that I used to be. If you would interview people in my past, you would find out that they have changed and regret their past decisions. If I knew then what I know now, I would still be a virgin. I still fight generational curses. But I tell you, the bus those curses rode in on stops here. It is over.

You have the same power to stop anything that you have inherited. Return it to the sender. If you don't want the package, don't receive it. Just because the dealer dealt the cards doesn't mean you have to take them. So many times we inherit iniquities from past generations. We see the patterns in our lives but we don't have to cut them out and make them fit us. Throw them away.

I must admit I have had some blows in the relationship area. I don't hate the men of my past. I love them in spite of the past pain. I just chose to turn my pain into gain. No matter what you face, there is always gain in it because all things work together for the good. I have met so many people who are facing or have faced the same issues I struggled with and it gives me the opportunity to minister and share my testimony about how GOD brought me out. I now have hope and a future. No test, no testimony. We all have choices. Choose to live and experience an abundant life inside and out.

Out of nowhere one day my father came into my hair salon and wanted to talk. I will never forget it. It was on a Saturday. He must have been waiting for my clients to leave. The doorbell rang and when I opened the door, my supposed-to-be daddy, whatever that word meant, was standing there. The moment I saw him, I made a choice to love him in spite of what he had to say. I was determined to love him even though he had caused me much pain and many tears. The truth of the matter is he is still my dad. When you see him there is no denial of that fact. I look like he spit me out.

I let him in and told him I had been fasting for about 30 days on a 40-day fast and here comes the missing link in my life at my door. I locked it because I was afraid he would escape just as he had done in the past. We began to talk. Every hidden issue I had with him came out that day. He surprised me. He answered all of my questions and made many apologies for his actions.

But just because he was saying he was sorry didn't mean that everything was peaches and cream. I had to try the trust factor. He had played hide and seek in the past and I could never find him. Believe it or not, he meant business this time. And I had changed a lot by then. I realized that there was a calling on my life and I was much more humble and open.

The key to winning is forgiving. I know you are saying, "What? Forgive?" I know it is hard to forgive but let me repeat, the key to winning is forgiving. I also know that it is not easy. Trust me, forgiving is a battle all by itself. I forgave my father but because of his past behavior we still have issues because of his denial to this day.

We became the perfect father and daughter. He took me around my sister, my brother and my stepmother. Believe me that is a whole 'nother book. We began to work things through. I found out why I did certain things. I love sports and all he did was gamble on sports. I always wanted to play golf. He and all of my uncles play golf. He has a great personality and like me is a people person. He loves walking and cooking and so do I. We are both songwriters and singers and we would often sing together.

I asked for his advice more and more but he got to the place where he would abuse his role as advisor and try to manipulate me. I struggled with that and with his trying to control things. Whenever he realized that I was interested in someone and he felt that they weren't good enough for me, he would run them away with a jealous jab. I had to reach the point where I would not tell him too much of my business.

I am 37 years old and my father and I have begun the cycle of disconnection, again. We are in another battle to the point of not talking regularly. He refuses to understand that all I have ever desired was for him to be in my corner. He just doesn't get it. I have always tried to show him my love. I witness him showing women and others what I have always wanted from him. My mom is deceased and sometimes I feel like he is also because of our disconnection. I have to trust GOD in this and seek my fatherly training from my Heavenly Father who will never leave and forsake me.

One thing I can say is that each time my father and I reunite, we are stronger than before. But, I hope this is the last round of this mess. I have to hold my hands and head up and keep my heart clean from unforgiving, envy, strife, jealousy and other blows that damage the heart, mind and body.

The best way to gain victory over an enemy is to keep your hands up in prayer and praise.

ROUND 5 POWER PUNCH

Death

Death is a powerful word and it also has a lot of power. Death means absent from the body, meaning no longer having breath in the body. Death is real and we all must embrace it in life whether we want to or not.

Death is a part of life that no race, color, age, or size can escape. It is the one thing in life that we all have in common. We cannot choose not to die but we can choose our destination after we die. The good thing about death is that there is life after we leave our earthly vessels. I know I will see Mama again in life after death.

Mama's death was painful, but it was good because it allowed me to see all that she had planted into me begin to grow and bring forth a harvest. Now I can train, nurture, plant and help escort people into their destiny.

Getting Off the Ropes

I have been in church all my life. I never stopped going. I was very active in church growing up. I would speak on many occasions at different events. I was also the one who would speak out if something didn't make sense. The more I spoke in the house of the God, the more I began to see a calling on my life.

In 1996, GOD began to really deal with me concerning ministry. There are times when your mama may call you and tell you to come here, but you don't answer. There are times when your daddy may call you and tell you to come here, but you don't answer. But there is something different when GOD calls you. You have got to answer, baby. You may tell yourself you're not going to answer, but you will find yourself in the belly of a whale.

Then you will say, okay, Lord I surrender all. I will do what you want me to do. I will say what you want me to say. I will go where you want me to go. I will bless whom you want me to bless. I will lay down my desire for your perfect will, not the permissive will, but the perfect will of the Father. There are many voices we hear in life but there is a difference when your Heavenly Father speaks.

I'll never forget when I actually heard the Lord call me. I had lost a lot of weight. I hadn't eaten for three days because I didn't understand what was going on with me. I was in the bathtub, when the Lord told me I was going to preach. I remember sinking down in the tub and crying. I thought, not me, there must be a mistake. Wrong house, wrong room, wrong Tongela.

I had spent close to 30 years at a church where there was a tight focus on the Word. We were taught primarily from Matthew, Mark, Luke, John and the Psalms. The pastor fed me spiritually what I needed at the time.

But I didn't have enough under my belt and I didn't know much about the Word in the beginning. All I knew was that Jesus rose and that I loved the Lord. I didn't know a whole lot about ministry. I didn't know the scriptures or where to find certain things. But GOD said I was called to ministry. As He began to knock on the door, I began to answer Him.

I went back to church the next Sunday and told my pastor that the Lord had spoken to me. I asked him to guess what the Lord had said. His guess was that I was going to preach. He knew my calling. We were close and he shared other things with me. But, he said he did not want to open a can of worms. Our church was Baptist, a traditional church, and women preachers were not allowed.

I didn't understand. If I come to you and tell you the Lord gave me a dream, and you tell me I cannot do it, even though I know and you know GOD told me to do it, then something is not right. The devil tried to kill my dream. Unfortunately, in ministry, you will be faced with dream killers, just as much in ministry and in the church as in corporate America or in the nightclubs.

I call the dream killers in the church the crab crew on the pew. When GOD elevates you and takes you to another level, the crab crew will try to pull you down.

The pastor knew I had a calling on my life, but he wouldn't let me preach. He would still let me do talks. Towards the end when I was going out of that church, I was flatfoot preaching. It didn't really matter to me. Preaching, teaching, talking—it all meant getting the word out and proclaiming.

Have you ever felt as though GOD has told you to do something that you knew you were unqualified, unschooled, and inadequate to do? That's how I felt. I said, "GOD, if you really have a calling on my life, then show me a sign that I know is from you." In the process, the Lord moved me out of my comfort zone, which was the church I grew up in, and placed me in unfamiliar territory at a new church home. This move put me in the position of really having to trust the Lord, hear His voice, and seek Him like never before.

But I still questioned GOD's decision for me to preach. How was I going to be a preacher? I talk just as flat and country. I said, "Lord, I know you aren't telling me I'm going to speak to the nation. I have no conversation." He said, "I need you to be real. As long as you are real, anybody, whether they're educated or not educated, will be able to relate to your message."

And I knew He was right. Sometimes we talk over folks' heads and our audience is limited and intimidated. But when you are real, you can tap into any audience. You are experienced in something. You have had a pain in some area.

When I look at my life, I have had some hard times in business and I have had some struggles but I have not really experienced lack. I have always had food to eat, shelter to live and clothes to wear. But there were times when I did not live in abundance and I'm not even there, yet. The key is to not allow your mess to mess you up. Believe and you will achieve.

Pastor Bady was the only man that saw great potential in me. This man encouraged me and pushed me. I learned more about prayer at his church. I got order. I got excellence. And I got built up. He ordained me in 1997 and I received my license. Pastor Bady was a dream builder.

The enemy constantly fought me because the pastor would have me read and I would stumble and not know the meaning of certain words. The devil would try to discourage me from doing the things that I wanted to do. But as I kept on reading, I prayed and asked the Lord the meaning of the words, and GOD began to reveal them to me and show me wisdom in the Word and in Webster.

I had never felt intimidated spiritually, but I did when it came to the natural. As I began to spend time with GOD and develop a more intimate relationship with Him, He elevated me even in the natural things, because I submitted unto him and the calling. Submission is important in life. Submission is powerful. In marriage we are to submit to one another. I learned to submit to my purpose and destiny.

The next church I went to was a very important part of ministry for me. It was the worst experience that I had ever had in a church in my entire life. It was very painful. But it was very important that I go to this place, because when I was there, I saw the warrior rise up in me.

I had already experienced prayer, excellence, and order. I had been motivated, exhorted, encouraged, and pressed to the next level. Pastor Bady began to stir the stuff up. I had to go to the next place to learn warfare. I couldn't be a prayer warrior and an intercessor without being faced with a war. If I didn't go through a war, how would I know that GOD would shield me and protect me?

The Good Book says we war not against flesh and blood so GOD allowed flesh and blood to make me think I was fighting against people. The enemy wanted me to think that I was in a war and that the people at the church didn't like me. But it was really GOD allowing it to happen to build up the warrior in me.

That is when I understood that I could fight in the spirit.

That is when I learned that the key to war is worship. That is when I really got on my face and stopped taking the attacks personally. I could have reverted to my old ways and gotten those folks straight. But I didn't do it. I forgave them because they did not know what they were doing. It was a character workout. God was building character in me. It was a thorn in my flesh to make me forgive the people who came against me.

The same devil in the street is in the church. The people in the church are the people from the streets. The same people who drive down the freeway are the same people you are going to see in the church. So don't think that once you get saved or get a call on your life that you're not going to deal with jealousy, envy and strife. They are waiting on you, baby. They have a pew. They have a whole section. They are in the pulpit.

When you know that GOD has a calling on your life, everything that you dealt with in the world is going to come at you. If it was lust, somebody is waiting for you with a lust spirit. Time you get saved and you start thinking you are holier than thou and you just got it all going on, baby, I promise you, the enemy is waiting on you. You are going to face the devil. Prepare to win.

My issues were men. They always bought me nice things and took me to nice places. They were drug dealers then. They weren't anywhere near saved. They did like many church members—go and don't have a clue.

Now I meet millionaires who say they love Jesus and tell me they can buy me whatever I want. You see, temptation never goes on vacation. That was the same demon that I faced in the world, so now that I'm in ministry, I've got to face that same devil. Buy me, buy me. I am already bought by the highest bidder, Jesus. I am sold out for life.

I left the church that had taught me so much about warfare.

I was wounded and fearful; wounded by drama that had taken place there and fearful because the enemy had confronted me, once again, by the one thing that made me powerless. This was the church where the pastor told the female minister that GOD could not use her because she hadn't finished high school. He told her that she couldn't make it and she wasn't going to the next level without furthering her education.

He wasn't even talking to me, but I felt the fear. It didn't even have anything to do with him. It was a set-up by the enemy to discourage me and it hurt me so. GOD won't use me and I don't have a diploma? And I'm already battling with that issue and here it comes right in my face? Once again, I was hit below the belt.

But GOD said, "I'm schooling you in the Holy Ghost, girl. You better get this. You better recognize." And I said, "But Lord, the pastor said…" GOD said, "I am your source. I am the only wise living GOD. With all thy ways acknowledge me and I shall direct you. Just trust me." So, I said, "Okay, Lord."

I dropped out of that church and went to Lakewood Church, the Oasis of Love. That is what I needed right about then. All I wanted to do was to sit down. In every church I had been to, I was close to leadership. In the church I grew up in, I worked with the pastor's aid. In the second church, I was working with the ministry. In the third church, I was the pastor's wife's handmaiden. I don't know how my mom felt as she entered her fourth marriage, but as I entered my fourth church, I sat down. I wasn't fixing anything and I didn't want anything to do.

The church that was always a comfort zone and a place of peace for me had been my first church—until I went to Lakewood. The first time I attended was the first Sunday of the year 2000. The first sermon I heard at Lakewood was about how Pastor Joel Osteen's father had dropped out of high school, built a church and got numerous degrees in theology—all without a high school diploma. It really ministered to me. It seemed like every Sunday, for the first couple of months that was all he preached.

Pastor Joel had just started preaching when his daddy died. I heard Pastor Joel tell his daddy's testimony on several occasions. The more I heard this testimony, the more I started to believe that I, too, could be a winner. I realized that if Pastor John Osteen could drop out of school and become Senior Pastor of a multicultural, nationwide church, with satellite churches across the world, I, too, by the grace of God could be raised up. I was encouraged to learn that Pastor John Osteen, after being saved, went back to school and finished with A's and B's. I was even more encouraged and inspired when I heard about how he hitchhiked to college and received his Master's Degree. What a role model. What a fighter. What a champion. It was obvious he was a winner

And then the hope came and the joy came. I got so free. My hopes were building and my faith was rising. As I sat there, the Lord began to minister to me and he said, "Now you're out of that other church. You're at Lakewood and this is an oasis of love." He said, "Now, this is the place where you're going to get yourself together."

One of the reasons I left the other church was because I did not want to be disobedient. GOD had told me to take a class called Purity with Purpose at Windsor Village United Methodist Church. After I finished that class, He told me to get my GED and then He would allow me to go to the College of Biblical Studies to show me that I had victory over a dropout spirit.

When I told the pastor that I was going to take the Purity with Purpose class, he told me it wasn't time. You see the key was, I was going to have to go to another church to take the class and the pastor didn't want me to do that. If it had been at his church, it would have been okay. But he thought if I went to another church, he would lose me. Control.

I wrote him a nice letter. I had a meeting with him and his wife and I said, "I know the Lord spoke this to me. And I do not want to be disobedient to your rules and regulations so, I'm going to go ahead and take this class and I'm going to leave this church." It was bitter, but the sweet part about it was, I obeyed GOD.

If you allow people to control you, your destiny can be put on hold. I knew GOD told me to do it and because GOD had so much other stuff for me to do, I had to do it. I just had to go to the next level. It didn't feel all that good but you've got to do what you've got to do. You cannot let man control you.

The Good Book says obey GOD, rather than man. Obedience is better than sacrifice. Some pastors will say obey them who have rule over you. But the highest ruler is Jesus.

I started attending the Purity with Purpose class, which was designed to help Christians find their purpose in life. It was here that my truth about being a dropout would come out of its hiding place. I decided to stop living a lie.

I told the woman who was leading the class that I needed to talk to her. She knew I had a successful business but I had to tell somebody about the mess I had been carrying for years that had become such a burden. I told her I had some luggage and it wasn't a small carrier. In fact, I had two suitcases. I told her I had to unpack those suitcases and unload some mess. I had to open it up and allow the Lord to come in and do surgery because I had a wound that had been lying dormant for a long time that had to be dealt with.

When she asked me what the problem was, I began to cry like a newborn baby. I revealed to her that I had dropped out of high school. I began to tell her the things that I had gone through. When I finished she said, "Girl, you got a story."

The class lasted 16 weeks and I didn't miss one week. That was like a diploma for me because when it came to reading and writing and certificates, I had never completed what I started. I would start and stop. I started beauty school, dropped out of that. I started Purity with Purpose, finished it. Thank you, Jesus. It built my hope up. I said, "I can do this."

I never got free to tell people that I was a high school dropout until I went to Lakewood. I took the GED test in July of 2000. I did it at home with no one's help. There were some parts of that test that were extremely hard for me. I locked myself in the house from Friday night until Sunday and I would not go anywhere until I finished. I fasted and I prayed. When I came off that fast, I had some Kentucky Fried Chicken and potato wedges, because I had completed my goal. I signed, sealed and delivered that paper by overnight delivery. I wanted to make sure they got my grade.

The man at the testing office said he would call me. I told him to call as soon as he got the paper and my test scores because I was very anxious. When he got the test, he called and told me not to worry, that I had done well. When I finally got the transcript, I screamed. I just hollered. He told me I had passed the test over the telephone, but I didn't want just an average pass. I wanted to ace it.

I made five 100's, a 90, a 93 and an 86. I did ace it. I made a 100 in math, which is my strongest subject. Even in something I didn't like to do, like reading comprehension, I made a 100. I promise you it was GOD. He had His hand on me the whole time. This had been a mountain in my life but even the little faith I had because of my fear and past failures moved that mountain. I felt I had mustard seed faith but even with that small amount, GOD was faithful to me.

The year 2000 was like a millennium for me. There were major breakthroughs in major areas. Things that I didn't think I could do, I was able to accomplish. It was a season of harvest. But I still had to keep climbing.

Even when you are in the ministry; even when you are a heavyweight champion; even when you are a millionaire or a movie star; even when you have break-ups, breakdowns or break-throughs; you will still have enemies you will have to face. If the curse that is following you is a dropout spirit, you still can go through dropout episodes. You still might have to confront and overcome and walk in victory.

In September of 2000, I went to the College of Biblical Studies. Guess what? I dropped out. The enemy was right there, trying to tell me that I couldn't make it; that I was still a drop-out; that my past was coming into my present and I could not go to my future.

The tormentor said, "I don't care that your future looks brighter. No one sees that but you. No one believes in you. You think you have accomplished something because of a piece of paper. That means nothing. It is not the real thing. It is not a real diploma. You forfeited that. It does not have the name of your high school on it. It's not real. Where are your graduation pictures, your class ring, your cap and gown? You will not be able to go to your class reunion. Right now, because of what you're still leaning on, you're not going to make it." That was when I knew it was a real fight and I had to win.

I did not give up. I had come too far. I had just jumped too soon. My timing was off. I was in a rush to go to the College of Biblical Studies because I wanted to be schooled by the world. I wanted to prove a point to myself and to others.

But GOD said, "Not yet. I'm going to release you. I want you to be schooled by the Holy Ghost. I want you to be schooled by your pastor, Pastor Joel Osteen. Sit down under him; this is your teacher right here." He said, "You want the paper because you want the people to see the paper. Stop trying to be a people pleaser."

GOD asked me, "What do you want, power or do you want the paper that has limited power?" I replied, "GOD, I want unlimited power. I want to walk by the devil and I want him to know I am there and I want him to flee." GOD asked, "What school do you want? Do you want to be schooled by the Holy Ghost or do you want to be schooled for a piece of paper that has limited power. I said GOD, "I want to be schooled by the Holy Ghost."

You see, GOD had blessed me with paper, which was money. One reason people get degrees is to increase their worth and make more money. I was blessed to make the money without having a degree. I began to get my mind together. I know I will eventually go to seminary or college one day. But right now, it is my season and everybody's season in the body of Christ to be focused on being schooled in the Holy Ghost.

Once you have been schooled and nurtured, and you have been on your face, and you have the ingredients of faith, love, joy, and happiness (the fruit of the Spirit), and GOD begins to minister to you, you will have something no school can give you. School cannot give you power. School cannot give you the anointing. School can only give you knowledge. But the Holy Ghost can give you power and more. You can't buy favor just like you can't buy class.

Sometimes pride comes in. You've been dropped out but you see the hand of GOD raising you up and you say, "Oh, GOD is really using me." People tell you, "Girl, you can preach (teach, sing, do hair, box)." And you begin to tell yourself that you're all that and a bag of chips. Close that door before it gets too wide open.

You have to stay humble. It is very important. If you come from nothing and you begin to see GOD working, you still have to stay humble. You still have to recognize that you still ain't all that. You're not but four days away from getting your GED.

So, you have to be really careful. You have to move when GOD tells you to move. His timing is always perfect. You have to move for the right reason and in the right season—for His glory. You must learn His rhythm. In rhythm there is timing. Moving and motion is the rhythm that produces miracles.

GOD always placed Peter and John around "people of power" even though they were "unschooled." But GOD said, "They may have the power in the natural, and they may have the schooling in the natural, but the power that I want to give you is in the Spirit and the knowledge that I want to give you is in my Word." I began to pursue the Word of GOD and to pursue GOD in Spirit. He began to raise me up and He literally schooled me.

It takes much discipline and determination. It's not just some hocus pocus. You have to take responsibility to make changes in your life. Trust me, in this ring you will be thrown many blows and punches. You must be disciplined and determined to win. *Always remember, it is a fixed fight.* No matter what the situation looks like, you go in a winner. Raise your scores and standards. Continue to excel and propel yourself to a new you and to a new level.

The things that have been revealed to me have not come from a book or from a pastor. Some revelation has come from a pulpit, but the power and the schooling came through pain, through frustration, through anger, through bad relationships and through dropout situations. The power and the schooling came from knowing that even though I fell down, I got up, again. Even though I dropped out, I was not knocked out. GOD was with me all the time.

There were times it seemed like I wasn't going to make it. It seemed like I could not go where my destiny called me to go. Why could everybody else go to college? Why could everybody else go to seminary? But GOD said, "I want all the glory and if you go to school, the school is going to get the glory. But if I school you, if you go through my school on your knees and on your face, I guarantee you will win first place."

See, what I had to be reminded of was that schools are limited. But there are no limitations when it comes to Jesus. I could have a line of initials behind my name, but it won't give me unlimited power. Only the Master Instructor can do that.

You can only go so high with a piece of paper, but you can go all the way with the power of the Holy Ghost and with the anointing of GOD. Jesus can take you where paper can't get you. The favor of GOD can get you in a place just because you are His favorite. The favor of GOD can get you in a place where a V.I.P. badge can't take you. You can be a world-famous celebrity and it can't take you where the favor of GOD can take you. It only comes through being schooled and spending time with the Most High GOD, the Only Wise and Living GOD.

Don't worry about what the world says. *Keep your eyes on the Word of GOD.* The world will change. The Word of GOD never changes. It is permanent. We focus on being schooled in books but the best book in the world is the Good Book. That is the map. That is the key to your destiny. That gives you your instructions and your directions on how and where to go. That gives you the precepts and the concepts, the do's and the don'ts.

If you want to know where to go and how to get there,

look in the Word of GOD. Too many times we look elsewhere. When we do, we get stuck. We stay stagnant. We go around looking funny. Tap in to the Word of GOD and seek the Lord while He may be found. GOD will make you a victor over everything that the enemy brings your way. Ask Him and He will do it. Seek Him and He will reveal secrets.

I am not telling anyone not to go to school or to college. If you want to go to college, go for it. It is an asset in life and I recommend it. I am saying that if you find yourself stuck, with no education and experience, God will help you through.

If you want to be a doctor, go to medical school. If you want to be a lawyer, go to law school. But if you don't have a college degree or any schooling and you are letting it hold you back, there is still hope for you. In all your ways, acknowledge GOD and He will direct your path in whatever you want to accomplish.

As I began to sit at Lakewood under Pastor Joel's teaching I was able to actually release, let go and get healed. I didn't have to go around anymore seeking a place to plant seeds. I believed I had the best soil in the entire world. The anointing on Pastor Joel is so pure. He's not perfect. He's just available so that GOD can be glorified.

Pastor Joel has shown me what someone unschooled by man's school, but schooled by the Holy Ghost can do. He had never preached before becoming a pastor. He doesn't have a PhD, but he has G-O-D. *And the Good Book says that with GOD, all things are possible—even when the odds are against you.* Negatives can be turned into positives.

Now if you're all degreed up and all dressed up and you got your briefcase, your Franklin planner and all the credentials, your paper and your schools — Morehouse and Spelman and Clark — will get the glory. And you will get some of the credit.

But if you walk in and become a pastor of a church after only working behind the scenes, and preach to thousands of people when you have never preached a day in your life, GOD gets that glory. When the church grows faster than ever before with hundreds of people coming to Christ each week, the glory goes to GOD. That is what happened at Lakewood Church and to Pastor Joel Osteen.

GOD is using Lakewood for Houston and for the nation. Pastor John's dream, his legacy, the mantle, and the anointing that was on his life have been transferred to all of his children who are all in full-time ministry. This was a man who was in poverty. This is a man who knew lack firsthand. This was a man who made a choice to stand even when others said he couldn't do it. He was not like his other sisters and brothers. He was not like his mama and daddy. He was determined to make a difference in his family.

The Good Book says that the Father is to leave an inheritance for his children's, children's children. As the Osteen children grew up, Pastor John Osteen had a gray box containing cash money which was used for lunch money and candy. As a result of Pastor John's growing up in poverty, he didn't want his children to experience lack in any area of there lives. As time passed on, he managed to overcome that generational curse of poverty by learning and applying The Word of GOD. He taught his children and modeled for them that it was GOD's will for there needs to be met and to live prosperous lives.

If Pastor John Osteen could change his poverty-stricken life and the lives of so many others, I know I could change my life. And that is what I intend to do. Even though my past was dark and dreary, and still there are times when I experience moments of bitter tears, I refuse to become a dropout for there is no way for me to be knocked out.

The power and the anointing of GOD will destroy everything that has come and will come up against me not just for me, but also for my children's, children's children. Not only will I change the ones after me, I am going to change this line, this generation. When the Lord blesses me, my sisters are going to get blessed. My niece is going to be blessed. The very stench of poverty will be destroyed. I am just waiting on the manifestation in the natural. I have already received it in my heart.

What are you waiting on? Is there something in your life that you need to overcome? Just stand on your feet and rise and possess and pursue the things of GOD and the things that you desire. How do you know that GOD can raise the dead if you've never been buried under anything? You don't have to be dead in a casket. Some people are walking around dead. They're buried under fear, depression, oppression, and lack. But even in all of that, GOD can still resurrect. Live and give and watch GOD multiply you.

ROUND 6 POWER PUNCH

Fighting the Enemy

Going after anything good is going to take a fight. You may feel like you are inadequate. You may feel like you're not equipped. But it is when the battles are won that GOD gets the glory. In the Good Book there is the story of Jehoshaphat who when faced with a war, did not put the people with the weapons up front. Instead, he put the choir on the front line. He said let the choir go before us and let's just worship Him with thanksgiving.

And as they began to worship the King of Kings, his enemies' army came up against them and GOD allowed a spirit of confusion to come on them and they began to fight against one another. Jehoshaphat never had to pull a trigger. They never had to raise a knife. They never had to curse or roll their eyes; all they did was worship.

If you never go through something, if you are never in a war, how do you know that GOD is going to fight your battle for you? Whenever you are faced with something in your marriage, you don't have to get mad at your spouse. What you do is get on your face and begin to say, "GOD, you are the Only One, Wise and Living GOD. GOD, you said that you ordained marriage. You're the One that said marriage is honorable in your eyesight. I didn't say it. You said it and your Word says that you hasten to perform your Word. Now do it. You said that you are my armor. You said that you are my shield of faith. I didn't say any of this. This is what your Word said." If you never go through something, you will never know.

Remember, whatever you go through, the key to overcoming is thanksgiving. In all things, give thanks. I dropped out of many things, but look at me now. I am writing a book that I know you are reading. Lives are being changed by my message which once was nothing but a mess.

You can have the same testimony. You can turn your mess into a message. Allow your sweet and sour to work together. Believe it or not, it tastes good. I like it. You may be fighting the enemy, sleeping with the enemy or working with the enemy. Change and watch the change in your life. Get a vision of victory. Start seeing in your faith sight. Then, your obstacle will become invisible.

ROUND 7

Who's In Your Corner?

There are four corners in a ring. There are four corners of the earth—north, south, east and west. There are four seasons—spring, summer, fall and winter. In my life's ring, no matter what corner I go in, there are player-haters there. I can go to the north, south, east or west and I can find player-haters. Whether it is winter, summer, spring or fall, player-haters are present wanting me to fall down and stay down.

As you begin to rise up, there will be player-haters in your life waiting to push you back down. It is wise to know who your haters are. Embrace them because they are powerless. When they show up, that is your cue to continue because you are on the right path to your destiny.

Let's look at the term "player-hater" a little more closely. A player could be someone on a team—your team. A hater, of course, is one who hates. You may have someone who from all appearances wants to be on your team and you let them on your team but the "real deal Holyfield" is that they hate you.

In all corners of my life, I have had players in my corner who turned out to be haters. They have had on my uniform, my colors and my logo. On the outside, it looked like we were a team. But behind the front was a hater at heart. Behind every cheer, they wanted me to hear boos. They wanted everyone to think they were on my team. They told me they wanted to win, but behind the scenes they betted on my opponent.

How can you be on my team when you are a player-hater at heart? *The Good Book says out of the heart flows the issues of the heart.* Blows flow out of a player-hater's heart. Think about the people in your life who are suited up in your uniform, logo and color, but behind the costume is a player-hater. It could be your mother, father, husband, wife, stepmother, stepfather, sister, brother, child, pastor, deacon, boss or neighbor. The list goes on. No one is exempted.

A player-hater uniform is one size fits all and player-haters come big, small, young and old. They come smelling good and meaning no good, mean as Joe Green. They want access to you and always expect an open door. Once they are in, watch out for their jealous jabs. Pay attention. A player-hater has a covetous mind. She doesn't want something like yours; she wants yours—your husband, your house, your career, your car, your money, etc.

In the fight called life, I encourage you to get used to hearing boos from the crowd and getting the blows from the corners. They are all a part of the journey to your destiny. You can't allow boos and blows to abort your purpose. I still hear and feel them but I am never knocked out of the fight. My faith and my face are so fixed on the promises that even though winds may blow and tears may flow, I am determined not to give up or look back. To sum it all up, I am in it to win it. How do I know I am going to win? Because it's a fixed fight. I am never a loser and neither are you.

I am glad to see the number of women who are excelling in life. Women are competing physically now more than ever. There are professional woman basketball players like my girl Cynthia Cooper, women boxers like Laila Ali, women coaches, commentators, firefighters, astronauts, golfers, pastors and women in the ministry.

I have had experience in all walks of my life with women. I have had to face opponents in nightclubs, in the pits of life and even a few in the pulpit. I would expect a fight in the club, on the corner, in the 'hood under a tree, or on the court with the score tied and one minute to play for the championship. I'm not surprised to find a fight in a crack house and in the boxing ring. But, I am having a problem in the church house and in our parents' house with sisters competing against each other.

Sisters, we need to get it together. We fight at mama's house all day and all night and go to church expecting it to be a safe place. But the church is often a boxing ring. I am kind of messed up because I don't know who is in my corner in the ring. I don't know who is on my side on the court. I really don't know who is on my side in the family, my job or my neighborhood. Worst of all, I don't know who is on my side in the church. Yes, I said the church.

I have had more blows, more stepped-on toes, more jealous jabs thrown at me in the church than in any other place I've been in my life. It never ceases to amaze me how alcoholics share the same whiskey bottle and how athletes on the basketball court share the same towel, while church folk can't even share the Bible. Now you know why some folk find it hard to come to church, and others refuse to come at all.

I am a bit bothered by our performance in what we call the house of GOD. Performers perform. It is a form of something, not the real thing. And that's what is going on in some churches. We are not real. We are not transparent. We hide in the corner of sin. We cover and masquerade under costumes. We slip and dip under the sheets and we hide in our closets. Our pastors are wearing mini skirts under pin-striped suits. Our priests are on the down-low and our principles don't know which way to go. Who are the people in our corners?

Many women are starting fights and sitting down while others are sitting down and watching fights. What will it take for us to come together in unity and not be so competitive outside of the ring, outside of the court and in the church? We compete with our clothes, our money and even our honies.

We are often on the same team striving to achieve similar dreams and themes in life but somehow we can't agree. *The Good Book says how can two walk together unless we agree.* Sisters, we need to learn how to walk and talk and go and grow together.

I have been Tongela, no one else but me. I have been used, misused and sometimes bruised in the ring on several occasions by women. I trust you. I believe in you. I cheer you. I promote you. I pat you on your back. But you stab me in my back. Who is in my corner? I am not saying all women are like this.

But I will say in the ring called life, you may encounter similar opponents. Don't be surprised by your enemies. They come in all shapes, forms and fashions. Keep your eyes open. They will attempt to steal a punch, kill your dream and destroy your reputation. Ask yourself who is in your corner. That is what I have learned to do.

One thing I recognized after each fight that I won, my worth increased. I became attractive to opponents because of my record of winning. When you are victorious the enemy always desires to bring you out of the fight. There is an attraction on a winner, on a celebrity, on an athlete. People are drawn to your success. Watch out for leeches from the bleachers and outskirts of life — leeches that run from the bleachers that want to suck you dry and never give you Gatorade. All they give you is Hatorade. Stay focused and watch grace carry you in the race, round and ring of life.

The Good Book says that even Jesus knew who was going to betray him and who would deny him. Know your enemy but don't stop. Your enemy might have your color on. Your enemy might be your color of skin. Your enemy might be in your corner geographically. But your enemy is still not in your corner wholeheartedly.

I have found that people who betray and deny you can be good workers. In spite of the hits and blows, I still have to love those who hurt me. Either they will change their ways or they will change their roles. The key for me is to not change in spite of the blows. I must continue to love. It is harder to walk in love while you are being mistreated. It is easier to go off and act like your enemy at a lower level. There is a test in it for you and for me. Can we love in spite of the sting we receive from the blow in the corner of the ring?

Just holler if you hear me. If I am stepping on your feet just say, "Ouch. Tongela, it is too tight; loosen up." It may be tight but it is right. You may have been the one who produced the pain or the one who received the pain. It doesn't matter. Evaluate yourself and your corner. This is key, men and women in the ring. Make sure you have a Master Trainer.

I am always faced with hits that have hitchhiked on a male and female bodily form. Their aim is to intimidate me, attempt to rape me, and abort my destiny. I call them blessing blockers. They are people or other influences placed in our way to block our flow of wealth, health and mental stability. They love to play mind games. Blessing blockers try to block the best for your life.

The way to defeat a blessing blocker is to give them what they don't want you to have and that is a blessing. The Master Trainer can show you how to do that. He will show you how to block the blow but in return allow the flow of love to run from you to your opponent. He can teach you how to allow good to cover the bad. *The Good Book says that love covers all sin*. It is not always easy. But you will find that what the enemy desires to destroy you with often buffs you and prepares you for the next fight. It works for the good.

I can't believe I made it through some of the fights I have had. Through some of them I figure out what the last encounter was all about—to prepare me for the fight I am in.

If not for the previous fight, I would not be able to take the current blow. I would not be able to stand and stare at my opponent square in the eye. Past pain and knockdowns are just training tools. It doesn't matter if they come from your friends, family, strangers or yourself. Allow love to flow and watch love block the blows and get you back on your feet again. My attitude now is it doesn't matter who is in my corner, male or female, bully or coward. It is a fixed fight and I will still win.

So, sisters and brothers, let us all get along. Let's cheer each other. Sisters, stop booing the brothers and start building each other up. Men, start respecting the women. We all need each other.

No matter what position or posture you take in prayer, always practice and exercise keeping your knees bent. When you are knocked to your knees, take out the time to pray. Praise GOD on your knees. When you get up from your knees and get off of the ropes, get ready for your comeback. What really happened in prayer was, you got fueled to fight and to finish by grace and not just by the bell.

In life, there are many things that can knock you to your knees like divorce, death, adultery, sickness, wayward children and more. Keep your ears open to hear your Master Trainer. Your enemy will always try to outtalk your Trainer. But you will never be ignorant of the enemy's devices if you listen to your Trainer. You will always have the upper hand on your opponent.

Normally, the enemy's goal is to continue to blacken your eyes so you can lose focus. That is what he did to me. He kept targeting certain areas of my life to get me off focus so that he could steal jabs and punches at any time. His ultimate goal was to steal my dreams, steal my self-esteem and blind me of my destiny and purpose.

I had to be honest in corners of my life's ring. I was always reminded of my stats, resume and track record. I had to remember where I was. I was in the ring of life, not in the streets fighting like I used to be. I struggled with my street fighting record following me into the ring.

Many times, our past tries to haunt us. Even though I have now graduated from an amateur, the enemy still tries to bring up my past record. Commentators give the details of my history, lie about my present and even try to predict my future. Before I ever fought in any battle, my biggest struggle was the battle in my mind, trying not to believe the lies, comments and predictions of people on the sidelines.

Sometimes I sit in the corner of the ring resting and preparing for the next round. I often pause and scan the crowd thinking if they only knew my pain and wondering how they would have taken the last blow that I took. Never look at someone else's position, posture or play and gloat about how you would have made different moves. You never know how tight the shoe is until you put it on.

People look at me and say if I was you I would do this or that. The fact is, they are not me. Don't compare yourself to people, paper or prestige. Be who you are and fight your fight to the fullest. Life's fight is seldom fair. Even though you have a title, position or piece of paper, neither determines your power. You see, I did not have a piece of paper, degree or diploma. That did not determine my attitude in life. My attitude and my gratitude in the ring were to win by any means necessary.

Don't become stagnant because you feel you are too old,

you don't have the "proper" credentials, or you failed before. Redeem your dream. Age ain't nothing but a number. Degrees can only go so far and failures can be turned into triumphs.

I can remember a time when my business was at its peak. I was pretty well-known and was fulfilling a portion of my dream. I had a home, a car and a good relationship. But behind the scenes, I felt powerless and was in pain. My title was business owner. I had a position in the church counseling great leaders with big titles, positions and degrees. They thought I had it going on and I thought they had it going on. We all felt powerless at times.

Think about what you are depending on to bring you power. Check your source. Who is calling your plays? Who is in your corner? Who is your coach? Who are you connected to? Find out where your power line is connected to. Make sure that every punch you throw in life's ring is a purpose punch. Let your aim be smack dead in the middle of your destiny.

I have heard family commentators repeat the plays and failed goals of past generations. Many began their plays but never crossed the finish line. Many stopped and dropped before the bell rang. My ancestors wrote goals on paper but never actually saw the manifestation. Not only did I have my track record haunting me but I had a history book filled with past family failures being read to me.

Every time I attempted to make a power play, someone would push play and a sad song would come on. I had to get to the point where no matter what song was playing, I forced myself to stay on course and maintain my rhythm and stay on beat.

When you stay on beat you automatically beat all odds that are against you. Stay focused. Redeem your dream and press fast-forward to get past the enemy's constant rewinding and reminding you of your past. When people press pause on you, rest for a moment, catch your breath and move on and watch GOD redeem the time.

In this book, I have included highlights of my past messes. I have beat the enemy to the punch. My mess is now my message. All things work together for the good. You can't stop people from hating you. Even though my opponent would often rewind, remind, play, pause, record and try to stop me, I have allowed everything to work for my good. Every negative play was turned into a positive and I am still positive and positioned to progress in power.

Though I was dealt an unfair hand I did not throw in the towel or give up. I played the hand that was dealt to me. How do you respond to an unfair hand, a hit below the belt, a jealous jab? You say you asked for oranges and got lemons? I will tell you what I did. With my lemons, I made lemonade and drunk it between each round of life. Chill and put it on ice. Stir it and just as the ice melts, watch your enemy disappear before your eyes like ice.

Come out of that corner. You can't hide. Rise and be healed inside and out. You won this battle. Your scars are turned into stars. Continue to shine.

ROUND 8

Knocked Down or Knocked Out

I had to live the life I lived to get to this very point. It was a set-up from the very beginning. It looked like I was decreasing, going backwards. But it was only leading to my promotion. The set-up was my dropout history. If I had never dropped out, how would I have known that GOD could put me back in the game, again? If I had never dropped out, I wouldn't be writing this book and millions of people wouldn't be set free. If I had not failed some tests and then retook some tests and then passed the tests, how would I have a testimony?

The only reason I have a testimony right now is because I fell; I failed some tests. I was disobedient to the will of God by fornicating (having sex with a man who was not my husband) in the wilderness of sin. I took things without paying for them. I failed to recognize that my blessings are connected to my obedience. My fall brought me to the realization that God really is a forgiving God and his grace is truly sufficient for you and me.

If the enemy came to me right now and asked me if I minded living my life all over again, I would tell him to shoot his best shot. I don't regret any of it because what I have been through has not been about me. It wasn't even for me. It was for GOD to get the glory. It was for someone else to be healed and delivered and set free to come out of whatever was trying to paralyze their purpose and plan. It had nothing to do with me, but I am reaping the benefits.

The Good Book says all things work together for the good. I don't care what it is. Even though it looked like my mama and my daddy abandoned me, the Good Book says it's working for my good. There are people right now who have been abandoned. There are people right now who don't have relationships with their mothers or fathers. I have a relationship with my dad right now. Where the enemy tried to destroy, GOD restored.

There are times we are knocked down, caught off guard and unprepared. GOD said, "You are going to know that I am a healer. No one, not your mama or anybody else will have to tell you. You're going to know it first class and firsthand." And the enemy said, "You're not going to be anything and I am going to make sure of it. I'm going to send a blocker in to keep you from your daddy."

But the Good Book tells me that it's all working for my good because if I ever become a mother, stepmother, mother-in-law or sister-in-law, I will know what to do. I will be able to tell my testimony. And because of the anointing that is on my life to be real in telling people my story GOD will be glorified and the people will be snatched out of the very hands of their opponents.

There is no way I could be where I am without Jesus. There is no way I would be able to go to the next level without Him. I am not talking rewards in the natural, because the most precious gifts, the jewels and the diamonds, are in the spirit. Before something can be worth something, it has to go through some fire. It has to be purified. And I know that it's not over. I will still go through some lions' dens and some fiery furnaces. But I know one thing. I am not by myself. I know GOD is with me.

Now I can see what I couldn't see in the midst of the storm. I didn't understand it. I wanted out. I didn't want the pressure. I didn't want the pain. But I had to go through it to see that it all worked together for my good. I promise you that I have shed, many, many tears. But I have learned that when I mix my faith with the power of GOD, anything can happen.

There was a time I was knocked down, hit and caught off guard with the death of my mom. Towards the end of her life, she backslid and dropped out of church. My sister and I sought the Lord and we fasted and prayed. My mom was an alcoholic. But my mom just didn't want to go to church.

I went on a fast for 21 days. When I came off of the fast, my brother called me and I told him that my spirit was telling me something wasn't right. I said, "It seems like I feel sickness coming. I see Pat getting sick but GOD is going to show himself. She is not going to leave this earth without accepting Jesus as her personal Savior."

The next day, I got a call that Pat had had a seizure and that I should get to the hospital. I didn't take it seriously. I went to take a bite of shrimp I was eating and I heard the Lord say, "It's critical. Put your plate down and go to the hospital."

I got to the hospital and Pat was in a coma. The doctors said she would not hear me. I said, "Pat if you hear me, if you accept the Lord Jesus as your Lord and Savior..." The doctor was telling me she couldn't hear me so she wasn't going to respond. I told him the Holy Ghost was working.

I said, "If you believe in your heart that Jesus is Lord and you accept him as your personal Savior and you believe that GOD raised Jesus from the dead, lift your left leg." In the depths of a coma, she lifted her leg. She never came out of the coma but she lifted her leg. GOD knew he had to do that for me. He had promised me that he would not let Pat leave without accepting Him. Because of my mess that I went through with my mom, I was determined not to let the enemy have her.

It was bitter. But the sweet part is that she is in heaven with

Jesus. What the enemy meant for bad, worked for my good. What I didn't know at the time of her passing was that a week before, she had gone to a church for a job fair. Before they started the fair they had altar call. My mom had accepted Jesus at the altar. I didn't know it. But GOD knew that the time was coming for Him to take her home. And he knew He had a promise that He had to fulfill for me. *The Good Book says the promises of GOD are yes and Amen.* He did that. I have to serve Him.

My mom didn't have burial insurance and we were not prepared for her death financially. But within 24 hours, everything was paid for. I shared a few words at Pat's funeral and I said, "You know what, we're not mad because the devil thought he had her but she got away." It may be hard to see the victory in a death situation. We miss my mom. But at the funeral, several people desired a closer walk with GOD.

After that, I knew my knees had to hit the canvas for real. The enemy wanted my family. I prayed for my daddy because he was out there. I prayed so much I got tired of praying. I said, "GOD, it's in your hands." My dad was attending Lakewood on a regular basis. If you come three times, you're automatically a member. I understood that. But I needed more evidence and GOD knew what I needed. You see, GOD will meet you where you are.

One Sunday I was worshipping and thanking the Lord with my hands up. My dad was sitting behind me. That day I didn't ask GOD to let him join. I had already asked Him years before to save him, and I opened my eyes and I began to see my daddy crying and walking towards the altar. I put both of my hands up. And I said, "GOD, you are faithful."

Your knees technically have to be on the canvas for your fall to be a knockdown. What a position to be in when in prayer and in battle. Miracles, comebacks and victories are produced in many knockdowns.

There is nothing like seeing your prayer request come to pass. There is nothing like seeing GOD change the bad into the good, the sour into the sweet. Just hold on to His unchanging hand. If He promises it to you, it is going to happen.

You see, my mom was an alcoholic. From the day she accepted Christ at the church job fair to her death the next week, she hadn't drunk one drop. She had asked my stepdad what he wanted for his birthday and he told her to do him a favor and don't drink. So, when she lifted her leg in the hospital in response to my question, she wasn't drunk. The enemy could not come in and say that she was.

We never know how or why we are going to be used. I'm sure if you asked me at five years old, I wouldn't have said I was going to drop out of school. I didn't know that was going to be my mess. I didn't know what was going to be the key to my future. Not only does this key unlock my doors, but it unlocks others' doors and answers questions many people may have about fighting and staying focused when all odds are against them.

ROUND 9

Victory Is Yours

There are people who have dreams that they have been holding on to for years. I read about a 99-year-old man who finally got his GED. Do you think he didn't always have a thirst and a hunger and zeal to want to reach that goal and realize his dream? What are your dreams?

Do you dare to dream that your loved ones get saved? Do you dare to dream that your marriage gets restored? Now that your kids are all grown and out of the house, do you dare to dream that you can go back to school and get that GED, Bachelor's, Master's or business degree that you put to the side years ago for family obligations? Do you dare to dream to be released from a dropout spirit, procrastination, laziness or low self-esteem that continues to keep you down?

You can have dreams all day long. But I dare you to move towards them. After you dream, you must go after it. Pursue the dream you see. If you keep dreaming the same thing over and over, it becomes a nightmare if never achieved. It doesn't matter what your situation is or what your dream looks like. GOD gives provision for your vision. But you have to make the first step and that first step is prayer and a plan on paper.

Many times when we dream we see ourselves in the dream at a certain age. Once we pass that age we feel that the dream is over. Never give up on your dream. It is never too late.

Sometimes you might have to take one step and then stand

still. While you are standing still, continue to pursue and persevere in prayer. It may seem like you are not moving in the natural or it may seem like you are just taking baby steps, but you may be moving in the spirit and the spirit can take you much further than the natural.

You can get on your face and pray for a change in California faster than you can get on a plane and get there. To get to New York from Houston, it takes about three hours by plane. You can bow down on your face and God can get there far quicker and give you a tangible miracle. And what would you want? Would you want your presence to be there or would you want the presence of GOD to be there?

Sometimes we focus on the natural too much when the supernatural is what is important. That's where the power is. That's where the dreams come to pass. *The Good Book says write the vision, make it plain and wait on it.* It's going to come to pass. Though it tarries, just wait. And the way it happens is through prayer.

As I begin to ponder closing statements for this book, I am reminded of three very important words: confession, preparation and procession. I know the dreams that have come to pass for me are due to my open-hearted confession to God, and my allowing him to wash away my sins in preparation for me to take procession of the promise. I now have a heart to win and a will to never give up.

As you can see, I haven't always been as strong in the Lord as I am now. I'm still growing as a child. I went to church regularly, and learned to pray, fervently. But I still did not have, a close, intimate relationship with GOD. Sin and satanic distractions had me bound in the past, but not anymore. I repented of my sins and chose to obey God's will. It was then that I realized my GOD-given dream, and now I am experiencing true freedom in my personal life and in my walk with God.

There are dreams inside of each of us. They are not hard to identify. Whatever you find a thirst and a hunger to do, whatever you get joy in doing is a dream. I can remember when I was going to women's prisons to minister and the joy I felt at seeing women get healed and restored and being able to release and let go.

Praying for people brings me joy. It was a joy for me to do hair. I was never mad doing hair. That's why it was easy for me to write the vision to have a hair salon. That was my passion. Where is your passion? What gives you joy and peace?

If you have a thirst for Sprite, then stop drinking Dr. Pepper. Go after that which you desire. If you know you wanted to be a golfer, but you're playing basketball, something is not right about that. Go after that which you desire, that you are good at, that you love doing, that you are effective in.

Now, it is probably going to cost you something. It is going to cost whatever effort you have to pay for you to move out of your past and present. Regiment your life so that you can get to your next place called palace provision.

There are people who have dropped out of situations because they didn't have the credentials. They felt inadequate. They got a job and stayed stuck in it even when they knew it was not what they desired. They stayed because in order to get the job they lied on their application. They are stuck because they know it takes something to move to the next level and many don't want to pay the cost.

Maybe they dropped out of school or have a felony. Maybe they fear taking tests, or fear the unfamiliar, or fear a different culture or race. They got the job they're stuck in because Uncle Bubba knew the person who was hiring. But the job that they really want has no hook-up. They don't know that the key is to look up. So they stay stuck in a hard place. They don't move.

They go nowhere. They don't feel like they know anybody. They are relying on the little source instead of The Source.

Your source is Jesus. Go to GOD and say, "Now, Lord, this is my petition, this is what I want to do. I don't know how you're going to do it, but I know you're going to work it out."

When I wanted to get my first salon, I went to Him. I said, "Lord, I don't know how I'm going to get in this place, but I know I'm going to get in there." I never had any doubt or fear. I called on people that I felt could help me behind the scenes. But I called on Jesus first because I knew that He had placed that thirst and that hunger in me to get the salon.

GOD is not going to keep letting a desire keep coming up in you if He has not equipped you to attain it. Whatever your dream is, if it is in the will of the Father and it gives Him glory, I know for a fact that you can have it.

If there is a dream in you, remember GOD put it there so it is really His plan in the first place. He is just using you as a tool to bring it to pass. The key is to persevere, go towards, go after, seek, search, and research. Don't just get out of the boat; walk on the water.

I read an article recently that the test to get your GED is getting harder. If you plan to get a GED, that news could discourage you and cause fear. It's not a bad thing that the test will be harder. You are equipped to pass. I told you not to focus on the voice of the commentator.

Some of us don't like challenge because it means we can't be lazy. We have to handle our business. We have to rise up. We may have to do a little more research. We may have to stay up a little longer studying. Go to the next level. Come out of the corner and move around in the ring of life.

Sometimes, you just have to go for it. Don't wait on anybody but GOD. But know this, as you begin to go, as you begin to seek, as you begin to look, what you want will not always be visible. GOD may tell you to walk into a room because He has 12 roses in there for you. You may walk into the room and not see 12 roses right away. You only see a bag of seeds, dirt and water. If you want the roses, you have to seek them. You have to search for them. You may even have to plant them.

See, you wanted to walk into the room and have someone just hand you the roses. No baby, you've got to go after those roses, plant and nurture them. But the good thing is you know they are in there. I know that there is a President, a CEO, a doctor, etc. in you. Plant and water those roses, see your dream come to pass and watch God increase you.

Don't let fear overcome the desire. *Faith fights fear.* When fear comes you have to say get back, get out of my face, back up devil. Keep fighting. Keep moving. It doesn't matter what it looks like or how long it takes. Even it you have dropped out ten times, keep getting up. The only way that you won't get up is an excuse. Excuses will keep you down. You've got to say, "Excuse me, get out of the way. I'm going to do this thing."

Then the faith will rise and once the faith rises, it will make you go after your dream, your plan, your vision, your marriage or your ministry. You must pursue, overtake and recover all, everything that the enemy has done to you. Get revenge against the devil. In the middle of the word 'revenge' is the word 'even.' The way to get even is get over. Get over and above your enemy, your failure, your loss, or your divorce.

Overtake the degree. Overtake the marriage. People have dropped out of marriages still loving each other, but because they dropped out, they don't think they can reconcile. I have talked to people who wanted to play professional football or basketball and they stopped because they got hurt. But then the Lord will rise up their children to play and their dream will live on. *The Good Book says GOD perfects those things that concern you.* GOD will perfect your dream as you begin to go after it.

There is power in the tongue. When you speak your vision, there is life, but be careful whom you speak it to. Watch out for the dream killers. If you know you have been a dropout for ten years and you decide to go back to school, don't go tell your cousin whose mama was a dropout and who knows that your mama, your daddy, your grandmother, and your great-grandmother were dropouts. You better be quiet.

In fact, you don't have to voice the vision. The Good Book doesn't say anything about speak the vision and make it plain. It says write the vision and make it plain. It doesn't say anything about writing it down and passing it out to every family member at the family reunion. On paper, you can consider it a contract with yourself.

When I wrote my vision down, I didn't go to Mama and say, "Look Mama, I'm going to do this." I just wrote the vision down and I knew it was going to be fulfilled. I've only shared it with those people close to me who I knew would want to go there with me. And the number was scarce. At some point, even some of those people turned on me. There are seasons in all of our lives. When someone's season is up with you, let him or her go. Make sure you have the right people as part of your SSS (Seasonal Support System).

Surround yourself with a good support team and wise counsel who can be a sounding board for your ideas. What really helped me when Mama passed away was I had a very good person on my dream team. She knew my dreams and not only encouraged me to reach them but she put some action behind her encouragement that included values and practical applications. Money could not buy what she did to prepare me for my destiny. It could not be taught only caught and I caught that blow with a smile.

I am still working on the third part of the dream I wrote down at 16. I am in the process of getting another duplex. I found one that was kind of pricey that I considered. It was owned by the same guy who sold me my first house. The most amazing part about it is how the enemy attacked us.

When I purchased my first house from this guy, it was the first house that he had bought and refurbished. He originally bought the house for $29,000. He spent about $30,000 to renovate. He sold the house to me for $95,000 and made a major profit. When I started to move in, I found all kinds of defects. I filed a complaint against him. This is how the enemy always tries to destroy. When it was time for court, I dropped the complaint because the spirit of the Lord told me to drop it. It was my flesh that filed in the first place.

When I dropped the complaint, the guy and I became friends again. Our relationship was restored. He now mentors me in certain areas of business. I could have not let that relationship be restored and I would have missed my blessing now.

You have to be able to take what the enemy meant for bad, and turn it into something good. That should always be our goal. If it's negative, let's make it positive. What would Jesus do? We wear that question on our wristbands and t-shirts, but are we really doing what Jesus would do?

As I move into the future, I am believing GOD for greater things. He is really enlarging my territory and broadening my borders and now it is time to launch out. GOD is using me as a water hose to flow through to water somebody else's lawn. It's not just about my lawn. I don't just want my lawn green. There are people down the street or across the world whose grass is not green. And if the Lord wants to use me to tunnel through so that he will be a well in a dry place, I just have to be the one and I am willing to be the one.

I began a nonprofit organization in 1997. Its mission is to edify, encourage, exalt and enhance women to maximize their fullest potential by revealing GOD's plan for divine healing in their hearts bodies, minds, and souls.

Before the organization was formalized, the ministry was just a study group. We would bring food, the move of GOD would come, the people would go home and they would be set free. Then the Lord said, "Get incorporated." That's when I felt challenged and I became unfaithful and fearful. I didn't know what to do or how to do it. So I did what a lot of people do in that situation; I procrastinated and hesitated and became frustrated.

I was being forced to come out of a box. Whenever it's time to bust out of a box life becomes a challenge. Anything that you have to bust out of takes force. You have to use some power. That is not always easy because there is a chance you will get hurt. But GOD has already shown me that He can heal my hurt.

I am at the place now that I don't have time to rest. I don't have time to sit back. It's time out for that. It's time out for excuses. My last excuse was the GED. There is nothing I cannot do now. O.H. Ministry is up and running and has impacted the lives of countless women. We have changed the name to Open Heart Center where surgery is being performed and healing and miracles are being manifested.

My dream is to go back to Fifth Ward, the very place where I dropped out of, and build something in the neighborhood in remembrance of Mama. It is important to me to go back to where my pain was and to heal others who are in pain.

I'm not the only one who dropped out of Fifth Ward. Because the Lord has healed me, He's going to use me as a vessel to go back to the ghetto and bring somebody else out. Jesus was from Nazareth and the Scripture says the question was asked, "Can anything good come out of Nazareth?"

Often, when I tell my testimony, I say can anything good come out of Fifth Ward? GOD brought me out and I know that *I'm a good thing because the Good Book says every good and perfect gift comes from above, therefore, I am a good thing.* The Good Book says that he that finds a wife finds a good thing. I know I am going to be a wife, therefore, I know that I am a good thing.

If GOD brought me out, don't you know there is somebody else He wants to bring out? It doesn't stop with me. He didn't bring me out to be high and mighty. He brought me out so I can go back and tell the people who have been dropped out that whatever they are under, there is power to bring them over. There is hope.

This book is to be the first of many GOD has inspired me to write. The titles are already written down. Before I began to write books I started telling myself that I was going to write books, even before there was a real thirst or hunger to write. I was just saying it because that's what everybody else who had reached a level of success would do. I know now that it was just another step in GOD's plan for my life.

I am still climbing. Sometimes I still start little projects and don't finish them. I have to be consistently vigilant and alert. But there is one thing that I do know, whatever I put my hands on to do will prosper. I have never completed anything that did not prosper. If it didn't prosper, it is because I stopped before the bell rang. Everything I have attempted to do in my life turned out successful, in spite of where I came from and the odds that were against me.

Even as a child when negative things were being said about

me, I knew that there was a dream, an aspiration to the things of GOD and I knew that I could do all things through Him. Even when I was in the clubs with daisy dukes on, you couldn't tell me I wasn't going to be anybody. Even when I was stealing, I knew that there was potential and purpose and GOD had a plan for my life.

It didn't matter what it looked like. It didn't matter what it felt like. I knew that GOD had impregnated me with a plan. I could have gone to the abortion clinic and not been able to abort my purpose. I was predestined to deliver this book and to turn my mess into a message. GOD planted a seed in me called destiny. He said, "You've got purpose, you've got a plan, you're going to bring forth this baby. This blessing is coming to pass and many births will come because of your obedience and transparency."

If I had said I couldn't make it, I would have been saying GOD wasn't able. But I had the victory long time ago. You have the victory. You are not a victim. You are free and the blood of Jesus is covering every desire, every plan and every purpose for your life.

The Good Book says the blessings of the Lord make it rich and add no sorrow. That means when GOD gets ready to do something, He is going to make you rich and bring peace, not sorrow. Where the enemy brings sorrow and condemnation, GOD said whom the Son sets free, is free.

That is why the Good Book says every good and perfect gift comes from above. Where the enemy brought the pain, GOD will give you the gain. The gain is the anointing and the power to bring somebody else out. We have the power over every serpent, over every scorpion, over every power of the devil. That means every dropout.

GOD says He always calls us to triumph. Whatever we are

in, we are more than a conqueror. A conqueror rules, reigns and has dominion. GOD says, in Him, you are more than that. You are more than just a conqueror. You are victorious. You are coming out to be an aid in the ring of life to help your sisters and brothers through their wounds in life. Rise up and be healed and watch your enemies be scattered.

ROUND 10

My Mess is My Message

My first name means angel messenger. To be a messenger you have to have a message. To have a powerful message that can show others that a dropout spirit can be overcome, you have to have gone through some mess. My mess is now my message.

No matter what I did in my life, I never forgot Jesus and He never forgot me. Even when everybody around me got caught doing the same things I was doing and went to jail, I never got caught. GOD was propping me up to let me know that His hand was upon me.

Before the foundations of the earth, before my mother was even born, before I came out of my mother's womb, He knew me. He ordained me. He predestined me. He planted purpose in me. GOD said, "You are my seed and you shall bring forth fruit in every season. You shall reap the harvest."

I know that I still have more to go through. *But, the Good Book says I can do all things through Christ.* So, I am not concerned. In fact, I really am not going through anything. I'm just taking a ride around the ring. That is the only way. With GOD all things are possible. Everything I do, everything I say, GOD has to get the glory. Even in my mess, He is with me. In my mess, He has blessed me and I was saved by grace.

The reason I have had to go into the prisons to preach is because of the things that I have done. I should have gone to prison, so GOD said, "You have a choice, you either go in here like this or I can allow and uncover everything that you've been through. You're going to serve time in jail. Figure out which way you want to do it. It's far easier to do it my way. If you rebel against me, I will allow the enemy to come in. I will harden the judge and I will allow things to come against you to let the people know that I am GOD." The reason that GOD covered me was He wanted me to know Him for myself.

The Lord began to speak to me. He said, "Your mess is your message, Tongela. I don't care what it looks like. Your test is your testimony. You may have flunked a test, but you will have an anointing behind every test I give you that you pass."

He said, "You think that this dropped out of school situation is going to kill you. It's for the enemy. What the enemy meant for bad, I'm going to turn around, and it's going to be good and it's going to work in your favor."

I told the devil, "You're going to pay me for this. I said, "I know that you orchestrated my dropping out of high school, but you're going to have to pay me." I said, "First of all, I am going to get an anointing behind this and help others. Second of all, you're going to pay me with some money because I am going to write my story down on paper and I am going to free other people and this book will be a bestseller." I will be on Oprah and other television shows. You have what you believe, say and do.

You watch GOD. This book is going to sell millions of copies. It's not about the money, but because the devil did it, he's got to pay me. And I'm not going to take 99-½, I want a hundredfold return for my pain.

The devil has got to pay me because of the way he tormented me and told me that I could not make it. He told me I wasn't going to be anything because my mama wasn't anything and my daddy wasn't anything. He said, "Your mama died living in an apartment. Your daddy is in an apartment right now." I said, "Devil, I am not leasing another day."

I haven't leased since 1995 and I am not ever going to lease again. *The Good Book doesn't say lease; it says possess.* I said I'm taking back everything. What my mom didn't have, I'm going to take her portion. What my daddy didn't have, I'm going to take his portion. I want my grandmother's portion. I want my great-grandmother's portion. I am going to have what GOD says is mine.

I am not going to be broke. I am not going to be busted and I am not going to be disgusted. I am determined to have everything that GOD promised me. I know it is not going to be easy. It will be a fight and I may have to face a few blows.

When Jesus went to the cross, it wasn't easy. GOD even wanted the bitter cup to be passed. There are times when I faced bitter and sour situations and mess I wanted to pass me by. But guess what, GOD said, "What you don't understand is, I'm working something out of you and when I work it out of you, you're going to be an instrument to work it out of somebody else."

It's not even about me, it's about Him, that GOD be glorified. *The Good Book says when Lazarus died, Martha and Mary were weeping and they told GOD, "If you would have been here this would not have happened."* GOD said, "This is not unto death but that my Father would be glorified."

There are times in our lives when we feel like GOD is not with us, when we feel GOD doesn't hear us. GOD never leaves. *The Good Book says GOD will never leave you or forsake you.* What I went through was not designed to kill me, but it was designed to build me so that GOD would be glorified through this dropped out situation.

There are people all over the world who have dropped out, who have been knocked out, who have fallen down and don't feel like they can get back up again. But the same GOD that was with Pastor Osteen is with you. If GOD made his dream come to life, he can make yours come to life, too. All you have to do is say, "I can make it." Many times, we let condemnation come in and we begin to compromise. Hold on to the promises of GOD and don't compromise. Just trust Him. He will make a bad situation work for your good.

A lot of things that go on spiritually, affect you naturally. People don't want to believe that. If there is a strong spirit of alcoholism in the lineage, they think it's just coincidence. Make sure you pay attention to the patterns. A spirit takes the past generations and its motive is to take you out, too. And if it can take the grandparents, it can take the mother, it can take the daughters, and it can take the children. It can go on and on until you overcome it.

You have the power to stop the pain and the curses in life. Make a decision to put up your stop sign against all generational habits. You are not an overcomer until you overcome that which comes after you. Have victory and it is under you.

The dropout spirit has been lingering in my family. Now is the time to get victory. You don't get victory until you expose it. If you don't expose it, you're still in bondage. If you can't talk about it, you still have issues. *The Good Book says they overcame by the blood of the lamb and the words of their testimony.* That is when you begin to walk in the victory. The anointing will gush out and you will begin to become free. You will tell your story to bring somebody else out of bondage.

We can't be in a pity party. We have to persevere. We have to keep moving. We know it's a mess, now let's turn it into a message. The key is to let people know what you've been through, what you have dropped out of. If you drop out, drop on your knees and pray and GOD will continue to pick you back up. So, you dropped out. You're not dead. You still have breath.

And while you have breath, your dream can come true. Until you leave here, you still have a chance to succeed. You are still a candidate for a miracle.

My life is a miracle by the grace of GOD and not by the bell. Just recently I learned a lot of things about my birth and about my family that I didn't know before. GOD kept it from me. He knew I couldn't handle it earlier in life. But He said, now is the time for it to be exposed. I didn't know there was incest in my family. I didn't know my mom had stayed in an unwed mothers' home when she was pregnant with me. But GOD knows the timing for everything and He knows when to put together the pieces to the puzzle.

Whatever you dropped out of and you still have a heart to pick up again, go for it. Make little steps if you have to. What is important is you're making steps toward your vision. A lot of times, we beat ourselves up. We don't allow ourselves to go to the next level. All that does is weigh you down.

That is a trick of the enemy to come in and discourage you and to keep you from trying. You will tell yourself that things didn't work out so maybe it was not what you were supposed to be doing, that maybe you should try something else. But in your heart, you know what you should be doing. Most people are not doing what they really want to do.

Anytime you build something it takes time. We don't want to go through the building part. We'd rather just get with somebody who's doing what we want to do. But we know our dream is to have it ourselves. It's easier to get on somebody else's bandwagon. That way, we won't have to build the foundation. We won't have to construct the frame. We won't need to outline the room, come up with the name. We won't have to go through all of that. We want it the easy way. It's quicker. We get more sleep.

Get off someone else's bandwagon and build your own. Come out of your comfort zone and go towards your dream. You have to stretch like a rubber band. If I took a rubber band and put it loosely around a small amount of hair, the band would not stretch. But if I add hair, the band will have to stretch.

We're okay with the size we are. But when it comes to stretching, we are scared we may pop. So we don't want to stretch. We don't want to extend and we don't want to go outside the box. We don't want to see our borders broaden. We don't want to touch that because if we do, we will have to go into the deep and into the unknown and face many changes. Changes are scary so many of us avoid them.

Because we have dropped out in the past, we're scared that if we try again, we may fail. If we failed in our youth, we can blame it on our youth and inexperience. But if we're 40 or 50 or 60 or more and we fail, we don't feel like we have an excuse. So we don't try.

But guess what, if you fail, you fail. Or like Esther in the Good Book, if you perish, you just perish. But it won't be because you did not pursue your goal. I feel like Esther. Baby, I'm out here now. I'm in the middle of the water. It is just as far to go back as it is to go to the other side. But I'm determined to go to the other side.

If I go back, it's the same distance as going forward. Either way I go, I've got water and I'm going have to walk it. Going backwards, I'm going to walk some water. Going forward, I'm going to walk some water. Going backward, I'm going to have some winds because people are going to criticize me for giving up and letting go. Going forward, I'm going to have some winds because people are going to criticize me for going ahead and holding on.

I know I'm going to face a storm, so I have to decide if I

want to face it backward or forward. Either way it goes, there's going to be a storm. Let's just make that plain. We are all going to have some storms. We are all going to have some adversity. That's life.

Choose your storm. Go forward and avoid living a life of regret. You may sweat. You may have threats but go after your dream. Come out of that corner, get off those ropes and watch GOD bring your dreams to pass.

Don't try to run from the devil, he is very present and you will face him. *The Good Book says the devil did not go to Job.* Jesus asked the devil, "Have you considered my servant Job?" GOD said, "Okay, Tongela, you need to be tested to see if you can go to the other side. I need to send a wind in to let you know I'm not playing. Either you're going to get up or get out. Either you're going to say something, or you're going to shut up. It's all on you."

Do you want to go forward to another level towards an increase? Or do you want to go back where there is decrease. Which one you want? Either way, it won't be easy. So you might as well go all the way forward.

Everything that I had to do I had to trust in GOD because I had no knowledge in anything I was called to do. I had to feel my way by faith. I could not lean on a degree, because I didn't have one. I could not lean on what class I went to or who taught me. I had no net. The only net I had was the Source.

Stop talking about your dream. Walk your dream. Now is the time for you to move. Stop complaining about your mess. Turn it into a message. It is time for you to throw some blows and finish this round of your life with a jab. Redeem the time and your dream. I believe in you. Your best is yet to come.

AND THE WINNER IS…

I always win. No matter what the situation looks like or who my opponent is. The end result is I have victory over my enemy. I remain open to the will of God.

In 2003, I referred my hair salon's clientele business to different entrepreneurs as a seed and am expecting a harvest. The non-profit organization that I started is still operating even though our focus has shifted on missions. My main focus is on writing and trusting God by faith to meet my needs. I am working on my next book entitled It's a Fixed Fight, speaking to public audiences, and ministering. I have also added assistant chaplain, loan officer and songwriter to my list of accomplishments. It took my past to produce this fruit and there is much more to come.

Hopefully, this book has encouraged you to jump, leap and conquer your obstacles and fears. We all have received and given some pains, letdowns, blows, bruises and punches in life. But we can't stop at what looks like a dead end.

Keep climbing, keep dreaming, keep loving, keep hoping, keep trusting, keep forgiving, keep winning, keep building and sooner or later, you will see your living has not been in vain. You are a champion and there is a winner seed in you ready to bloom and blossom and be seen on the earth.

I know have victory over what use to have me bound. See how the tables change? The key is to never give up and never let go. No matter how hard it gets. No matter your age. No matter your present status. I am victorious today because I made a choice to add my sweet time and my bitter time together and it has worked out for my good. You do the same and watch what you get. When you mix all that mess together you will receive a *miracle on the move.*

I am still fighting but I go into the ring knowing that it is a fixed fight. I always win no matter what the situation looks like or who my opponent is. The end result is I have victory over my enemy. I look back over to my life and know that all things work together for the good. **Be good. See you in the next round and book!!!!!!!!!!!!!!!!!!!!!!**

About Tongela Clark

Tongela Clark, author, motivator and entrepreneur, is a positive, magnetic force on earth to be reckoned with. Her life's journey from "ghetto girl" to champion is a story of inspiration and healing for all. A born fighter, Tongela entered life's ring as a Winner, Leader and Champion and has maintained those titles despite the corners of the ring she has been in. She has a never-ending faith to the things she is called to do against all odds and past pain. Tongela's famous words are, "My mess is my message and I believe it will touch the world". Get familiar with her name. Tongela Clark will be known among the nations as a change agent. And The Winner Is...Tongela Clark!

ORDER FORM

Dropped Out But Not Knocked Out
(Paperback version)

Please pay $18.95 (plus $5.00 shipping & handling) through one of the following options:

Online Orders:	www.nomoredropouts.com
Mail Orders:	Ready Writers Publishers P. O. Box 88352 Houston Texas 77288-8352
Fax Orders:	713-526-7336 (*credit card orders only*)

Name _____

Address_____

City/State/Zip_____

Daytime Phone_____ Evening _____

Fax_____

Email Address_____

Number of Books_____

Payment Method: (check one)
_____ Check (personal/company) _____ Money Order
_____ Credit Card (choose one)
_____ Master Card _____Visa _____ Discover

Card Holder Name _____

Billing Address (if different) _____

Card Number _____

Expiration Date _____

Card Holder Signature _____
                    (**Must have signature**)

Shipping Name* _____

Address_____

City/State/Zip _____

*Note: No shipments will be made to Post Office Boxes.